THE DOCTOR A

AND OTHER

BY DYLAN THOMAS

ADVENTURES IN THE SKIN TRADE
and Other Stories

A CHILD'S CHRISTMAS IN WALES
illustrated by Ellen Raskin

A CHILD'S CHRISTMAS IN WALES
illustrated by Fritz Eichenberg

COLLECTED POEMS

THE COLLECTED STORIES

THE DOCTOR AND THE DEVILS
film and radio scripts

THE POEMS OF DYLAN THOMAS

PORTRAIT OF THE ARTIST AS A YOUNG DOG
Autobiographical stories

QUITE EARLY ONE MORNING
and Other Stories

REBECCA'S DAUGHTERS
A film scenario

SELECTED LETTERS

UNDER MILK WOOD, *A Play for Voices*

THE DOCTOR
AND THE DEVILS
AND OTHER SCRIPTS

by

Dylan Thomas

New Directions

CONTENTS

THE DOCTOR AND THE DEVILS

by

Dylan Thomas

from the story by
Donald Taylor

THE DOCTOR AND THE DEVILS

I

MORNING.

Music.

From a long way off, we see a deserted road winding downwards from a hill-top.

Huge sky, slow clouds.

A small black figure appears at the top of the road, and moves downhill. A small black figure with another darkness billowing around it.

Now we see the downhill-approaching figure as a top-hatted man in the wind. From our distance he is still the mystery of a man, alone in a blowing morning on a lonely hill-top; still the shadow, not the recognizably featured substance, of a man.

Closer now, we see that he is a youngish man in severe professional black; and his long cloak is the other darkness around him.

Closer still, we see his body and face as he strides down towards us. He wields his stick like a prophet's staff. We see the deep-set eyes behind the large spectacles; the wide sensual mouth tightened into its own denial; the wild fringes of hair blowing from under the sides of the stiff hat-rim; the coffin-shaped forehead; the insatiable, and even predatory, curiosity of the bent-forward head.

Suddenly he stops, looks down.

Now, with his eyes, we see the City that lies below him. An early nineteenth-century City, its crossing, twisting patterns of roofs at so many different levels, its streets and houses dangerously clambering, scaling, falling down from the steep hill, its patchwork of threading alleys, its compact wilderness of little archwayed courts and closes, sunless dead ends, market spaces surrounded by tumbling top-heavy tenements, hovels, cottages, pigsties . . .

I

And now, from behind him, we see him stride on, top-hat and
stick, towards the City; towards the rising sigh of city sounds, the
mingling and slowly loudening voices of people and bells, the
noise of hooves and wheels on cobble stones, and street cries
unintelligibly distant.

DISSOLVE to

2

CITY MARKET-PLACE.

And up come the City sounds.

The straw-strewn cobbles of the Market are crowded with stalls.
Stalls that sell rags and bones, kept by rags and bones. Stalls that
sell odds and ends of every odd kind, odd boots, bits of old meat,
fish heads, trinkets, hats with feathers, broadsheets, hammers.
Stalls with shawls. Stalls like ash bins. Anything that is market-
able, to the very poor.

Pigs and chickens grunt, root, cluck, and peck among the straw
heaps and the refuse, getting in every one's way though no one
notices or cares.

A heaped high hay-cart rumbles over the cobbles.

The doors of the shops and the public-houses are open on to the
Market, and singing comes from inside some of them, and outside
some of them stand men and women drinking.

And men and women lean, drinking, against the stalls.

There are many, many children, some very old.

Among the children, the butt of their noise, is a humpback with
the smile of an idiot.

And across the Market the man in cloak and top-hat is walking:
black and purposeful among all the turbulent laziness, among the
talkers, the hawkers, the old leaners, the drinkers, the shrill children.

We move with him.

Two men whom we see we will remember later. With earthenware
tankards in their hands, they are standing almost in the middle of
the Market. One is tall and very thin; the other squat, barrel
chested. The tall one is hollow-cheeked, corpse-pale, with jerky,

2

inconsequent gestures; the short one full and ruddy-faced, knob-nosed, surly, slow-moving.

We see that the tall one is laughing: at nothing. We hear his laugh: a high-pitched snarl, an animal noise. The squat one pays no attention, but curses the whole Market with his scowling eyes.

We see a woman pushing a barrow heaped with rags and hucksters' scraps, and another woman trailing behind her.

We hear the first woman's cry as she turns into a side alley:

Rags and bones . . . rags and bones . . .

she cries.

And then the cry of the second woman:

. . . Cat-skin . . . human hair . . .

The faces of the two women also we shall remember.

Rags, rags . . . rags and bones . . .
Cat-skin . . . human hair . . .

The tall man mimics the cries.

A hawker passes, crying her cry of:

Fresh herrings . . . fresh herrings . . .

We hear behind her cry the high yelping mimicry of the tall drinker.

The man in cloak and top-hat moves on.

And the noises of the Market fade as we

DISSOLVE to

3

CITY SQUARE.

The man in cloak and top-hat is walking through the trimly treed garden in the Square towards a large building.

We follow him into the building.

4

HALLWAY OF ROCK'S ACADEMY.

As he walks through the Hallway, a Porter, in black coat, black trousers, and brass-buttoned waistcoat, approaches him. He is a little man with a very pale face.

PORTER. They're here, Doctor Rock.

Rock stops.

> ROCK. Indeed, Mr. Forsythe? Who or what are 'they,' and
> where is 'here'?
>
> PORTER. The specimens for the Anatomical Museum, sir,
> are in the Museum.
>
> ROCK. How fortunate they are not in the gentlemen's cloak-
> room. I should hate skeletons in all my cupboards.
> Thank you.

Rock walks to the end of the Hallway, opens a door, goes through.

5

SMALL CLOAK-ROOM.

Rock hangs up his hat and cloak, very neatly, puts his stick in a
stand, and turns to look at himself in a full-length mirror.

We see, in the mirror, that he is wearing a long, dark coat, immaculately tailored, an ornate, embroidered waistcoat across which gold
chains hang in festoons, a high cravat, higher than is the fashion
of the gentlemen we shall see in future scenes, with its folds passed
through a diamond ring, a prominent shirt-collar, delicately plaited
cambrics, watch-seals and pendants, dark trousers, shining boots,
a gay waist-band.

At all this excellence he looks with approval; he preens himself, he
flicks off invisible dust.

Softly he says to his reflection:

> ROCK. Well, Thomas. To work!

And he crosses the Cloak-room to another door, and opens it, and
walks through.

From the Cloak-room door we see into:

6

THE ANATOMICAL MUSEUM.

It is a very large room.

Around the walls are anatomical specimens mounted and labelled.

4

There are specimens in glass cases, many unmounted specimens, and a great number of packing-cases of all sizes.

Assistants are unpacking the cases.

All over the floor are bones; the skeletons of birds, beasts, reptiles, fishes; odd fish; fossils; osteological curiosities; pickled monsters; brains in jars; the scattered treasures of a static, silent zoo.

Rock, some distance from his assistants, is opening a case and throwing aside the top layers of straw.

We *TRACK TOWARDS* him.

He takes a little skeleton from the case: the skeleton of a baby or a monkey.

A man's voice is heard.

> MAN'S VOICE. Good Morning, Thomas.

Rock looks round.

PAN ROUND to door through which a heavily built, elderly man is entering. His hair is close clipped and iron grey, his demeanour severe, his face unaccustomed to smiling.

Now, from the door, we see him cross over to Rock.

They shake hands.

Rock still holds the little skeleton under one arm.

> ROCK. Doctor Manson! You see me to-day, sir, with one foot in the grave. Now, where is a chair?

He looks around the Museum room.

> ROCK. Perhaps you could make yourself comfortable on this case of . . .

He glances at a label on a packing case near him.

> ROCK. . . . stomachs of cetacea. I am *sure* there was a chair here yesterday. I remember it distinctly . . .
> MANSON. You probably talked its hind legs off. Don't fuss around me, Thomas. I shall sit here on your stomachs.

Manson sits on the near case.

Rock puts the little skeleton carefully down. He goes on unpacking specimens throughout the conversation.

MANSON. You look well. Odd, but well. How is your wife?

ROCK. Well, and not at all odd, thank you, sir. Oh, the doctors' wives still cut her in the street, but fortunately they resemble their husbands at an operation: they cannot cut anything properly. And you, sir?

MANSON. I am an old man. You should not ask old men how they feel, or they will tell you. I am old, like Doctor Hocking.

ROCK. Doctor Hocking was in his second childhood before he was adolescent. When he is your age, sir—a good age —he'll be old as the grandfather of a tortoise, take a week to put his boots on, a fortnight to suck his bread and milk, and a month to make up his absence of mind.

MANSON. You still do not approve of the distinguished Professor of Anatomy in our University.

ROCK. I still do not approve of stupidity and inefficiency, and sycophantic compromise, and pretentious, intolerable airs and graces.

MANSON. [Unsmiling, as throughout.] You speak too highly of him.

ROCK. He has become a professor on no wits at all. If he were a half-wit, with *his* self-assertion he would be known as a Scotch Sophocles.

MANSON. I am thinking of retiring, Thomas.

ROCK. If you leave your School of Anatomy, sir, you con-sign the medical reputation of the City to a man who reads his grandfather's lectures for his own and dissects like a labourer with a pick.

MANSON. I have no intention of leaving my students to *Doctor Hocking*. I would rather continue lecturing myself, toothless, on crutches, with my beard to my boots. I founded *my* School to keep the teaching of Anatomy away from hacks and drudges and medical impostors, crammers, and quacks. [Slowly, emphatically.] My successor must be a person of precision, method, vigilance, and expertness.

6

ROCK. In this City?

MANSON. I have found him.

ROCK. Oh, in heaven, sir, not here.

MANSON. In a museum.

ROCK. In a mummy-case?

MANSON. No, standing like a fool in front of me, with a leg under his arm.

Manson looks at Rock. And from his eyes we see Rock standing, a plaster leg under his arm, among the specimens he has unpacked from the cases; Rock staring back at Manson.

And we *TRACK BACK* to see Rock and Manson still, silent, in the great room surrounded by bones and bodies, like men in a spilt graveyard.

DISSOLVE to

7

A ROOM IN ROCK'S HOUSE (henceforward to be known as ELIZA-BETH'S ROOM).

It is an intimate, comfortable room.

A fire is blazing in the deep fire-place.

There is a table with sewing upon it.

And another small table with books.

Rock stands at the long window of the room, looking out.

Coming closer to him, we see, through the window, the roofs of the City.

It is dusk in autumn.

A woman comes in. She is young, small, fair, with a candid, tranquil face.

She is carrying a tray with biscuits and a glass of milk on it.

She stands for a moment, looking at Rock.

Then he turns.

ROCK. I never heard you come in, Elizabeth. You're a witch

7

in a white apron. Downstairs you keep a little instrument,
no bigger than a baby mouse, that can hear my brain ticking
and my heart beating.

Elizabeth puts the tray down on a table.

> ROCK. [Gently.] Shall I tell you my news now? Or shall
> I kiss you first . . .

Elizabeth smiles calmly up at him.

> ELIZABETH. Yes.

He kisses her.

> ROCK. . . . and ask you what you have been doing all
> day . . .
> ELIZABETH. Oh, the ordinary things.
> ROCK. . . . and how our little boy behaved . . .
> ELIZABETH. He's asleep now. He said his prayers, and then
> he said there was a tiger in his bed.

She smiles.

> ELIZABETH. Tell me your news now.
> ROCK. Do you remember Doctor Manson? Stern as a judge
> and solid as a mountain. When I was a student, he had
> the bearing and the voice of a god surrounded by the angels
> of logic.
>
> Now he's old, and ill. He knows death. He can hear
> it growling and scratching around him now, like a dog
> after a bone.
>
> He wants me to take his place. Do you know what that
> means? A whole School of Anatomy outside any influence
> but Manson's and my own. All the work I have ever
> wanted to do, I can do there. Can you see me as another
> St. Hilaire, my dear, another Cuvier? . . . Another old stick-
> in-the-mud, maybe, with bees in his bald head . . .

The room is growing slowly darker.

> ROCK. I said 'Yes' to Manson. Are you glad?

Elizabeth nods.

> ROCK. When one burns one's boats, what a very nice fire it makes.

He looks out of the window, over the roofs in the gathering darkness, Elizabeth near him. He speaks almost as though to himself alone.

> ROCK. What can spoil or hurt us now? Nothing, nothing, nothing. Nothing out there. . . .

He makes a gesture towards the dusky City.

> ROCK. My future's here.

He raises his hands, palms upwards, then draws them back towards him, inviting Elizabeth.

She moves to him, and he takes her hands.

> ROCK. And some of it is in your hands. Oh, I am happy to-day, Elizabeth, happy and tired.
> I am tired of the dead! . . .

He puts his arm around her, draws her close. Together they stand at the window. His hand moves along her bare arm.

FADE OUT.

FADE IN

8

LECTURE HALL OF ROCK'S ACADEMY.

Rock is on the platform, lecturing.

Another younger man sits at a small table on the other side of the platform.

The amphitheatre is crowded with students.

Rock, as a lecturer, shows a rare felicity of movement, now reminding us of the slow and graceful minuet, then the quiet pose or soldierly *attention*; and these again are succeeded by the rapid gesture. After each diversion of his subject he readjusts his spectacles, draws up his gay waist-band and then, presenting a steady front to his class, resumes his prelection.

9

ROCK. I stand before you, gentlemen, as a lecturer in Anatomy, a scientist, a specialist, a *material* man to whom the heart, for instance, is an elaborate physical organ and not the 'seat of love,' a man to whom the 'soul,' because it has no shape, does not exist.

But paradox is inherent in all dogma, and so I stand before you also as a man of sentiment, of spiritual aspirations, intellectually creative impulses, social convictions, moral passions. And it is in my dual capacity of scientist and sociologist, materialist and moralist, anatomist and artist, that I shall attempt to conduct my lectures, to expound, inform, illustrate, entertain, and edify.

Our aim for ever must be the pursuit of the knowledge of Man in his entirety. To study the flesh, the skin, the bones, the organs, the nerves of Man, is to equip our minds with a knowledge that will enable us to search *beyond* the body. The noble profession at whose threshold you stand as neophytes is not an end in itself. The science of Anatomy contributes to the great sum of all Knowledge, which is the Truth: the whole Truth of the Life of Man upon this turning earth. And so: Observe precisely. Record exactly. Neglect nothing. Fear no foe. Never swerve from your purpose. Pay no heed to Safety.

For I believe that all men can be happy and that the good life can be led upon this earth.

I believe that all men must work towards that end.

And I believe that that end justifies any means. . . .

Let no scruples stand in the way of the progress of medical science!

Rock bows: a curt, but studied bow.
The students rise.
And Rock walks off the platform.
The other man on the platform makes a gesture of dismissal to the students, then follows Rock.
And all the students suddenly begin talking as they move down the Lecture Hall.

9

HALLWAY OF ROCK'S ACADEMY.

Rock and his companion on the platform are walking through the Hallway towards a door under the stairs. They open the door and go through. We follow them, through the open door, into a

10

SMALL CLOAK-ROOM.

It is a bare, dark room. A few pegs on the wall—Rock's cloak and top-hat hang from one—and a table with a water jug and a basin on it.

Rock rolls up his sleeves, very circumspectly, as his companion pours water into the basin.

We hear, from outside, the noise of the students.

> ROCK. [With a nod towards the noise.] What do they talk about afterwards, I wonder? Do they repeat one's words of golden guidance? Or make disparaging remarks about one's waistcoat? I think when I was a student we used to tell one another stories: they were anatomical, too. Ah, thank you, Murray. . . .

Rock begins to wash his hands in the basin. Murray takes off his coat.

> MURRAY. You agree with all you said?
> ROCK. But naturally.
> MURRAY. 'The end justifies *any* means'? That is—to say the least of it—unscrupulous.
> ROCK. Then do not say 'the least of it.' Say 'the most': that it is *honest*.

And Murray begins to wash his hands.

> ROCK. You're coming to my dinner, of course? I can

11

guarantee the cooking. Only the conversation will be half-baked and only the politeness overdone.

MURRAY. [Smiling.] Of course . . .

ROCK. . . . Do not trust an elder sister to choose one's company for one. Annabella will never believe I am properly grown up and so sits me down next to an elderly lady whose conversational ability would disgrace a defective three-year-old, or else closets me with a deaf historian so far advanced into the next world that he can only dribble and splutter in this.

MURRAY. [With a kind of tolerant affection.] Dinner will be a monologue, as usual, Thomas. I can't think how you ever manage to eat or drink anything at all on those occasions. . . .

ROCK. I eat during the yawns.

Now he has finished washing. He adjusts his coat-sleeves. And Murray helps him on with his cloak.

ROCK. I *loathe* all Dinners with a capital 'D.' Why can't I have a *quiet* meal with a small 'm' and a large port?

MURRAY. Oh, but William! A Dinner to Celebrate the Opening of the New Session of Doctor Rock's Academy!

ROCK. I wish it were still Rock's and Manson's Academy . . .

He puts on his top-hat. Murray passes him his stick.

ROCK. [As though to himself.] . . . Poor Manson . . . [Suddenly in a different mood.] If Annabella hasn't invited at least one Duke I shall be so surprised that I shall have to ask one myself. And throw in a drunk baronet for bad measure.

Good night, Murray.

He walks to the door of the small, dark room.

MURRAY. Good night. Sleep well.

ROCK. Don't be a dam' fool. . . .

Murray smiles after him as Rock goes out.

And from Murray's eyes we see Rock walk down the Hallway
towards the main door, which is opened for him by the Porter,
Tom.

II

DINING-ROOM OF ROCK'S HOUSE.

On the large, shining table of the large and handsome room the
candles are lit in their heavy silver candlesticks.

The curtains are drawn.

The furniture of the room is good and solid.   There is little orna-
mentation.

At the table sits a woman, writing.   There are coffee-things near her.
We TRACK TOWARDS her, from the door.

And, close, we see that she is a woman of about forty, with black
hair combed sternly back, strong features, straight unrelenting
mouth: a woman of determination, who knows her own mind
and, though she may not like it, will always speak it.

She is writing, with severe, upright pen strokes, on large white cards.

There is the sound of a door opening.

She looks up from her writing, and says:

> ANNABELLA. Oh, Thomas.   Can you spare me a moment?

And now, from a little way behind her, we look at Rock standing in
the doorway, hesitant, top-hat in hand.

> ROCK. A hundred, my dear Annabella.   All my time is
> at your disposal, except when I am working or eating or
> drinking or sleeping.   And so on.
>
> ANNABELLA. Then come in and close the door.
>
> ROCK. I *was* going upstairs to work.   I had thought of
> completing my Observations on the Structure of the Stomach
> of the Peruvian Llama to-night.
>
> ANNABELLA. I doubt if such a creature exists.   I think you
> invented it as an excuse.   And besides, if it does exist, it
> probably has no stomach.

13

Reluctantly Rock comes in and closes the door behind him. He approaches the table.

ANNABELLA. I want you to look at the invitations, that is all. I may have forgotten someone.

ROCK. Oh, fortunate someone!

Annabella hands the little pile of cards to Rock. He looks through them, idly.

ANNABELLA. There is no need to be contemptuous of a celebration in your own honour. It may well be the last if you continue to go around the City capriciously insulting every one, and writing absurd letters to the papers about every subject from salmon-fishing to astronomy, and preaching perverted nonsense to a lot of credulous youths and calling it the new philosophy.

ROCK. I smell vinegar in the air to-night.

But now he is looking through the cards again, and this time not idly. He speaks in a changed voice.

ROCK. Why are not Doctor and Mrs. Gregory invited?

ANNABELLA. Mrs. Gregory will not sit at table with *her*.

She makes a little gesture of her head towards the door. Rock gives no sign of having heard or understood.

ROCK. And the Nicolsons?

ANNABELLA. No self-respecting body would sit down at dinner in the presence of . . .

ROCK. [Interrupting, quickly, but in an expressionless voice.] . . . my wife.

ANNABELLA. You can't think that you can outrage every convention and not suffer for it. You married her for better or for worse; and it's worse. I have never understood why you didn't keep the girl as your mistress in some other part of the town.

But no, you have to bring your shabby amours back into the house and *legalize* them.

People have long memories. They don't forget that you

14

disgraced your name, *and* mine, and defied every social
decency when you married . . .

But Rock, silent, is walking to the door, opening it, and going out.
He pays no attention to Annabella. She is left standing at the
table, her sentence unfinished.

12

STAIRWAY OF ROCK'S HOUSE.

Rock is climbing the stairs. As he climbs we hear the voice of
his mind.

> ROCK'S VOICE. . . . When I married Elizabeth. When
> I said, cool as ice, one morning—cool as fire!—'Elizabeth
> and I are married. Oh, the shame and horror on the faces
> of all the puritanical hyenas, prudery ready to pounce
> and bite, snobbery braying in all the drawing-rooms and
> breeding-boxes, false pride and prejudice coming out of
> their holes, hissing and spitting because a man married
> for love and not for property or position or for any of the
> dirty devices of the world . . .

We see him, from below, climbing up, disappearing round one
winding corner, then appearing again out of shadow. And the
voice of his mind grows softer and, slowly, fades.

13

ELIZABETH'S ROOM.

Elizabeth is sitting near the fire, nursing a young child, as Rock
comes in. She looks up. She sees the controlled fury on his face.

> ELIZABETH. Thomas. You have been losing your temper
> again.

He crosses to her, and looks down at her and the child.

ROCK. Not this time. No, my dear, society has been losing its temper with *me*. And you.

ELIZABETH. Society. That's a lot of people.

ROCK. Oh, Annabella is the priestess of the whole genteel rabble. She speaks for all the slanderers and backbiters from here to hell.

ELIZABETH. [Gentle, as throughout.] Was it you and me again?

ROCK. Again.

ELIZABETH. It makes people so angry, still. They think that if they don't *show* they're angry *all* the doctors and lawyers will be marrying market girls and housemaids . . .

ROCK. It would do them good. I wish all the mummified lawyers would marry women of the streets and breed howling families of thieves and vagabonds. I wish the professors would marry their cooks and breed *proper* children, not more little scholars in diapers.

ELIZABETH. Oh no, that wouldn't work at all. You are famous. People want to look up to you. They can't do that if you insult them by marrying below you.

ROCK. Below me! Love is not below me! What am I? An insensible pedagogue, cold-blooded as a herring, with my nose permanently buried in a body? A mincing old maid of a man with . . .

ELIZABETH. No, dear. Which of your friends have been refusing to meet me now? I've only met a few of them. I thought they were very nice and they got up when I came in and called me ma'am . . .

ROCK. I do not need any friends. I prefer enemies. They are better company and their feelings towards you are always genuine. No, it is only that some overweening and underbred women, the wives and tormentors of unlucky doctors, have contrived to tell Annabella that they would not accept our invitation to dinner.

ELIZABETH. Oh, but they *must*. It's very important. You must be at your best. I want them to respect you. You must tell your sister to send off all the invitations, and at the foot of the ones to the ladies who won't accept because of me you must tell her to write, very nicely, that I won't be able to be present at dinner because I am indisposed.

ROCK. I shall cancel the dinner.

ELIZABETH. You 'll do nothing of the sort, Thomas.

ROCK. Then I shall write to tell them that their inability to accept our invitation is obviously due to the fact that they suffer from swine-fever, and that I appreciate their delicacy in not wishing to spread it.

ELIZABETH. You 'll tell Annabella exactly what I 've told you. And now that subject is all over. You haven't asked anything about your son. He couldn't go to sleep to-night. He cried and cried. He was frightened. I 've had to nurse him to sleep.

Rock kisses Elizabeth. He touches on the forehead the child in her arms.

ROCK. Good night, little boy.

And we *TRACK PAST* Rock towards the window, out of the window and into darkness.

14

Music.

Night.

A graveyard.

Three muffled figures skulk down the graveyard path. One carries a lantern. By the lantern-light we see the shapes of the grave-stones on either side; some of the graves are thickly spiked and railinged round. And by this light we make out the appearances of the silent, shadowy figures.

One is very tall and thin; he wears a top-hat. One, also top-hatted, carries some heavy implements; the lantern, for a moment, flickers his way, and we see the shape of a spade, the coils of a heavy chain. The lantern-carrier is a very short man.

Now the lantern-carrier stops at a new grave, and lowers his light. The grave is only a tidy heap of newly turned earth; no stone stands at its head.

We hear the whisper of the lantern-carrier:
> Here it is. This is the one.

The spade-bearer puts down his implements. We hear his whisper:
> Hallelujah.

And the tall, top-hatted man whispers:
> Go to it, Mole.

The short man begins to dig at the end of the grave earth.

And the tall one, looking carefully, slyly, around, whispers again:
> Quiet as death to-night.

And the one who carried the spade whispers in return:
> Praise be the Lord.

The short man digs on. Then, putting down the spade, he whispers:
> The chain!

The tall man hands it to him. We see that the chain has a large hook at the end. We see it thrust into the hole the spade has dug. And we hear the noise of steel knocking on wood.

The chain, in the hands of the short man, wriggles above the earth like a snake.

Steel grates against steel.

The short man whispers:
> It's a hard clasp they've put on the coffin.

His companion whispers:
> . . . The unbelievers.

And the tall man whispers:
> Break it with the spade, then. Hurry. The cold's got into my bones.

The short man pushes his spade through the earth. Spade against steel. The ripping of wood.

The tall man whispers:

> Careful.

And the chain is lowered again.

And slowly, out of the earth, comes the head of a man, and then the shrouded shoulders, hauled up by the hook of the chain.

The tall man whispers:

> Easy, easy. Don't wake him.

Slowly the three men raise up the fourth.

The arm of the dead man drops, stiff, against the lantern.

The lantern goes out.

And suddenly, to loud gay music, we *DISSOLVE* to:

15

INTERIOR OF TAVERN A.

On a bench in a corner sit three men. No one sits quite next to them, though the tavern is crowded. We recognize them as the three men of the graveyard. All three are drunk, though solemnly as befits men whose business is death.

The very tall top-hatted man (Andrew Merry-Lees) is a cadaverous clown; a deacon of the drinking-cellar, a pillar of unrespectability.

The other top-hatted man (Praying Howard) has an almost benevolent, almost sweet and saintly, appearance run to seed and whisky.

The short man (Mole) is very hairy; almost furry, like a mole.

They raise their tankards to each other.

> ANDREW MERRY-LEES. To the dead!
>
> PRAYING HOWARD. To the Surgeons of our City!

They drink.

Now we see, sitting quite close to them, the two men of the Market-place. They are listening hard, but cautiously, to the other three.

> MOLE. It's been a good month. I'm thirsty.
>
> PRAYING HOWARD. A blessed month.
>
> ANDREW MERRY-LEES. Subjects like penny pies. Plenty

19

of 'em. I'm thirsty too, Mole. I've drunk three pints o'
gin. And I'm goin' to drink *three pints more* . . .

PRAYING HOWARD. Careful, careful, Andrew, you 'll get the
taste for it.

And the three of them croak and laugh, without smiling, like three
carrion-crows.

And the two men of the Market are listening all the time.

The short, squat man beckons, secretly, with a stubby black finger,
to an old woman, all rags and bones, standing drinking near them.

Coming closer, we hear his whisper:

Who would they be with all that money for the drink?

The woman looks, with frightened eyes, at the croakers in the
corner. Then she whispers:

Andrew Merry-Lees, and Praying Howard, and . . . [her
voice goes softer] . . . the Mole.

And the squat man questions her again, in a rough, Irish whisper:

And what do they do for a living, my lovey?

She answers, in a sharp whisper full of fear:

Body-snatchers.

He makes a movement as though to cross himself, then lets his hand
fall, and looks at his companion.

We see the thin side-twisted lips of his companion frame the syllables:

Body-snatchers.

They look at each other as the camera *TRACKS BACK* to show
the whole tavern and the three solemnly croaking, laughing men
in the corner.

DISSOLVE TO

16

DINING-ROOM OF ROCK'S HOUSE.

There are eight gentlemen at table.

The port is being passed.

Through the general conversation we hear:

GREEN. I was sorry to hear that Mrs. Rock was indisposed, Thomas. Only once I had the honour . . .

FIRST GENTLEMAN. Nothing, I hope? . . .

ROCK. [Shaking his head.] . . . Serious. . . . The child. . . . The weather . . .

SECOND GENTLEMAN. [Nodding in the direction of Murray across the table.] I was asking Mr. Murray, purely out of academic interest, why body-snatchers are known as Resurrectionists. He was polite enough to excuse my morbidity so soon after dinner, but . . .

MURRAY. I'm afraid I was rather uncertain myself. Thomas can tell you.

GREEN. Thomas knows *every* answer. I sometimes suspect him of prearranging the questions so that his encyclopaedic information can come rolling 'spontaneously' out.

ROCK. You overestimate me, Doctor Green. I can answer every question only *after dinner* when people are usually not in a position to verify my facts. But Mr. Sinclair's question is too simple. The removal of a body from the walled pre-cincts of God's Acre was viewed by the superstitious and the credulous as nothing less than an interference with the plans of Providence and the Great Resurrection. So the poor ghoul of a body-snatcher became a 'Resurrectionist.'

THIRD GENTLEMAN. If by the superstitious and the credulous you mean believers in Christianity, Doctor Rock . . .

ROCK. Sir, I did not say a superstitious and credulous Christian any more than Brahmin or Buddhist or Wor-shipper of Elephants. If I say, in conversation, that I know a woman who is opinionated, vicious, and ugly, I *do* distrust the man who immediately says: 'Sir, you are talking about my mother!'

THIRD GENTLEMAN. If Logic itself came to dine with you, you would give it an excellent dinner and then try to strangle it. All I wanted to say was that as a Christian I

21

deplore the sacrilege of digging up the dead for anatomists
to dissect.

FIRST GENTLEMAN. [To no one in particular.] I wish I had
retired with the ladies.

ROCK. I am no platform drummer, no hawker of slogans,
but I say that the Resurrectionists who dig up the dead and
sell them to the Anatomical Schools are a direct result of the
wrongness of the Law. The Law says that surgeons must
possess a high degree of skill. And a surgeon cannot
acquire that skill without working upon dead human beings.
But the Law also says that the only dead human beings we
can work upon must come from the public gallows; a very
uncertain, and meagre, supply. Legally, the hangman is
our one provider. But he would have to hang all the *liars*
in the City or all the men who are unfaithful to their wives,
before there would be sufficient subjects for us. Therefore,
we have to obtain our bodies illegally.

I myself, last term, had to pay out five hundred guineas
to the Resurrectionists.

Rock drinks.
Murray passes the port to the Second Gentleman. The Second
Gentleman fills his glass.

SECOND GENTLEMAN. [Aside.] What very good port they
provide in a mortuary these days . . .

But Rock now has the attention of the whole table.

ROCK. Do not suppose for a moment that, even after dinner
and in one of those mellow, argumentative moods in which
one would try to prove that black is white or that politicians
are incorruptible, I regard the Resurrectionists as anything
but the vicious human vermin of the gutters of the city; in
fact, a pack of devils.

But as the Law says 'No' to our need, to the need of pro-
gressive science, so up crawl these creatures to satisfy that

need *against* the Law. The same applies to every city, though *ours* is rather more fortunate than most; it is *full* of perverted blackguards.

GREEN. [Provokingly.] If you dislike so much the Law that applies to your own science, Thomas, why did you become an anatomist rather than anything else?

ROCK. There was more body to it

FIRST GENTLEMAN. You would make our City sound to a stranger like Sodom or Gomorrah. . . .

GREEN. It *is* a seat of learning, after all, Thomas . . .

ROCK. And the bowels of squalor. Look any night at the streets of this 'cultured city.' Observe, with academic calm, the homeless and the hopeless and the insane and the wretchedly drunken lying in their rags on the stinking cobbles. Look for yourselves, sirs, at the beggars, and the cripples, and the tainted children, and the pitiful, doomed girls. Write a scholastic pamphlet on the things that prowl in the alleys, afraid to see the light; they were men and women once. Be proud of *that* if you can.

In the silence that follows, Murray rises to his feet.

MURRAY. If you'll excuse me, gentlemen, I must try to brave this—'*terrible* city at night.' You'll excuse me?

At a smiling nod—for Rock has again, suddenly, changed mood— Murray bows and goes out of the room.

ROCK. [At his most jocularly donnish.] And now, gentle-men, no more such talk from me.

SECOND GENTLEMAN. Oh, surely, not a little entertaining gossip about cannibalism, for a change?

ROCK. No, no, no, not another word. Or, as my friend Murray would say, 'Let us change the subject.'

LONG SHOT of the dinner table, Rock at the head, waggishly professional.

17

Music.

Night.

Murray is walking along the middle of the street. On both sides
of the street are many ragged bodies, of men, women, and children.
Some are stretched out asleep; some are sprawled drunk, their
hands still clutching a bottle; some are huddled together, like
large, dishevelled birds, for company and warmth. A few have
not managed to reach the comparative shelter of the sides of the
street, but lie, ungainly outcasts, snoring scarecrows and men of
garbage, across the cobbled middle. Over these bodies Murray
steps quickly, carelessly.

CUT to

18

Another humanity-littered CITY STREET, with Murray walking
along it.

CUT to

19

DOORWAY OF ROCK'S ACADEMY.

Murray is knocking at the door.
The door opens slowly, only a few inches at first, then we hear a
husky voice from within.

> VOICE. Och, it's you, Mr. Murray.
> MURRAY. Open up, Tom.

And the door is quickly opened wide. Murray goes in.

20

Murray stands waiting in the gloom of the Hallway while Tom closes
the door.

Tom has a candle in his hand. He moves hurriedly in front of
Murray and leads the way through the darkness down the Hall.

> TOM. I thought it might be another *subject*, sir, at this time of
> night. There was one brought in only an hour ago . . .
> [In a whisper.] By you know who. Andrew and . . .
> MURRAY. Shut your mouth.

They reach a door at the end of the Hall.

Murray opens the door. Tom, with his candle, scuttles back into
the darkness.

21

DISSECTING ROOM OF ROCK'S ACADEMY.

Night.

A large room, cold, clean, and echoing.

Tables and slabs.

Anatomical diagrams on the walls.

On one of the tables we see an array of shining instruments: knives,
saws, choppers, and long sharp steel tools.

The room is lit by one flickering gas-jet.

Two young men stand at one of the tables.

On it we see, half in shadow, a shrouded body wrapped in sacking.

Murray is coming into the room.

> MURRAY. [Brusquely.] Evening, Brown . . . 'ning, Harding.

Murray crosses to the table. He unwraps the sacking, flings aside
a few soiled white cloths, lowers his hand in between them.

For a moment there is silence.

> MURRAY. Stand out of the light, will you?

Suddenly he flings back the cloths, and straightens up.

MURRAY. [In angry undertone.] Ugh! This is a week old! Why can't the fools bring something fresh? Don't they get paid enough? Might as well dissect a dog dragged out of the river after the fishes have been at it. Come on, let's go and have a drink in the market. *That*'s not worth pickling. Come on.

He walks towards the door, opens it, stands waiting.

Harding lowers the gas.

And out of the dim room the three of them walk into darkness.

And out of the darkness comes loud, gay music, and we are in:

22

INTERIOR OF TAVERN B.

Shouts and laughter, and a wet dribble of singing.

The benches are packed tight with beggars, hawkers, cheap-jacks, drunks, street women, rogues, and slummers.

The rough tables are crowded with tankards and bottles, stained with spilt drink.

At the open doorway, children rabble together.

Moving slowly down the room, we pass the two women whom last we saw crying 'Rags and bones' and 'Cat-skin' through the Market.

In their bedraggled shawls and cock-eyed bonnets they look as though they might have been made out of their own wares.

Moving slowly down, we pass, near the two women, a beautiful girl of about twenty years who has spent nearly half of them trying to defeat her beauty. She is giggling, half tipsy, at some unpleasantry.

Moving slowly down we pass Andrew Merry-Lees and Praying Howard. Sober as churchyard worms, in their corpse-dusty top-hats, they are trying to cure the hiccups of Mole—who sits, small and furry, between them—by pouring drink from a tankard down his throat.

Moving slowly down, we reach Murray and the two young students,

Brown and Harding, with tankards before them. They are, all three, a little tight and talkative.

> BROWN. Refined gathering to-night.
> HARDING. Too refined for old Murray after his hurly-burly with the great. How did the dinner go?
> MURRAY. Thomas was on top of the world.
> BROWN. Gracious, loquacious, insulting, exulting . . .
> HARDING. [Overtopping him.] . . . drastic, bombastic, charming, disarming . . .
> BROWN. [Not to be outdone, with extravagant gestures.] . . . avuncular, carbuncular.
> HARDING. What did he talk about at dinner, apart from sex and religion and politics?
> MURRAY. Body-snatchers.

Harding, with a 'Sh!' of warning, gives Murray a dig with his elbow, and nods up the room to where Merry-Lees and the Mole are now solemnly pouring whisky down Praying Howard.

As Murray looks in their direction, so he sees the beautiful girl and beckons her over to him.

Beautifully unsteady, she approaches. Brown and Harding squeeze up to make room for her beside Murray.

> MURRAY. Sit down and drink with us, sweet Jennie Bailey, my lovely charmer. . . .

CUT to the two Market women looking with undisguised dislike at Jennie Bailey, Murray, and the two students, who are now drinking and laughing together.

The first of the women, she who cried the cry of 'Rags and bones,' is soddenly morose, a coarse slattern and drab.

The second woman, she who cried the cry of 'Cat-skin,' is a bawd and virago.

The first woman says:

> Look at Jennie Bailey, the lady. Drinking with the doctors. Look at her, Kate.

KATE. I'd like to be putting my nails in her eyes. . . . I saw that Bob Fallon looking at her yesterday. Mind your step, Nelly.

NELLY. She won't be young for long. Another year and the men won't look at her. She's the sort that grows old in a night.

I seen your Mr. Broom looking at her, too. Showing all his teeth.

KATE. She wouldn't go with Fallon or Broom, not she. Look at her. Not when there's money.

CUT to CLOSE SHOT of Murray and Jennie. They are sitting close together. Brown and Harding have moved away from them, further down the table.

MURRAY. Why can't we meet in another place, sometimes, Jennie? Anywhere else, not always in this damned tavern, with all the sluts and drunks staring at us.

JENNIE. Where else *could* you take me, sweetheart, except for a walk in the fields—and in winter too! Kissing in a hedge in the snow like two robins.

MURRAY. We could find somewhere to be together.

JENNIE. Loving in the lanes, with all the trees dripping down your back and the thorns tearing your petticoats, and little insects wriggling all over you—oh no! Or sitting holding hands in your lodgings all the evening, and your brother studying books in the other corner! [Softly.] You know you could come home with me.

MURRAY. And you know that I won't. I *can't*! Don't you understand that I couldn't go back with you there. Not there, in that house. I don't want to think of you in that house, ever. I don't want to think of the others, and your smiling at them and letting them . . .

JENNIE. Oh, the 'others' don't mean a thing in the wide world. They're *different*. I'm for *you*. Come back; now. I'll tell Rosie you're staying and . . .

MURRAY. No. No, Jennie. Please. You're *beautiful*. Come

away. Come away from everything here. Are you never going to say 'Yes' to me, even if I ask you a thousand thousand times! I'm asking you again, Jennie . . .

JENNIE. [Gaily.] Oh, a fine young doctor's wife I'd make. Wouldn't the ladies love me? 'And from what part do you come, Mrs. Murray?' 'Number 23 Pigs' Yard. Your husband used to call on Wednesdays.' . . .

CUT to the door of the tavern, where the two men of the Grass-market, the tall, thin, always half-dancing one, and the squat one, are standing.

They look round the room.

They see Kate and Nelly, and make their way across the crowded, swirling bar towards them.

The tall one crackles his way through the crowd, jumping and finger-snapping, a long damp leer stuck on the side of his face.

The squat one elbows his way through, now sullenly truculent, now oily and almost bowing.

They stand over their women.

And the squat man says, ingratiatingly and yet with an under-menace:

> Can you buy a little drink for us, Nelly darling? We're thirsty, love.

And the thin man says, in his high, mad voice:

> Can you buy a little drink for Fallon and Broom, Fallon and Broom. . . .

He makes the grotesque movements of drinking, still finger-snapping, one shoulder higher than the other.

> NELLY. There's money for two more and that's all. Here, buy 'em yourself, Bob Fallon.

She tosses Fallon a coin. And as he catches the coin and shoulders the few steps to the bar, Broom reaches for Nelly's drink. Nelly makes as if to snatch the tankard back, but Broom suddenly shows his teeth and pretends to snap at her.

29

KATE. Ach, leave him be. Broom s got the devil in him
to-night. He'd bite your hand through. I know him.

By this time Fallon has returned with two drinks, and hands one to
Broom, who attacks it hungrily again.

Fallon, from under his heavy, hanging eyebrows, stares around the
bar. Suddenly he sees Merry-Lees and the two others.

FALLON. [To the women.] There's the three . . . [His
voice lowers.] . . . snatchers we see in the 'Old Bull.'
They're swillin' the drink again. Must've digged up
another to-night.

He turns to look at Broom, who is staring at the three Resurrectionists
with glinting, unseeing eyes.

FALLON. Fourteen pounds for a corpse they get when it's
digged up new. . . . Fourteen pounds! . . .

BROOM. [In his high, loud voice.] Fourteen pounds for gin
and pies . . .

KATE. Hush! you mad dog. . . .

NELLY. There's no more left.

She gets up and goes towards the door. Fallon follows her, Broom
and Kate behind him. As they move through the bar to the
door, we hear Fallon whine:

FALLON. Come on, Nelly darlin', scrape up a penny or two
for a drop for us . . . There's plenty of ways, lovey . . .

23

THE MARKET-PLACE, OUTSIDE TAVERN B.

Moonlight.

The noise of the tavern swirls in a hiccuping gust out into the street.

The Market stalls are shrouded like dead-carts.

And the doors of other pubs and houses are open, staining light
out on to the cobbles.

People stand at doorways, up to no good.

People and other pigs flop on the strawed cobbles.

Nelly walks to a barrow just outside the pub and takes the handles. The barrow is heaped with rags.

Fallon, Broom, and Kate follow her as she begins to push the barrow through the moonlit Market.

Suddenly, with a yelp, Broom leaps on to the barrow, sitting bolt upright among the rags.

> BROOM. [In a high, gay snarl.]
> > Broom
> > In his carriage and pair . . .

Nelly takes no notice but doggedly pushes the barrow on.
And sullenly Fallon walks at the side, Kate trailing after him.

> FALLON. Fourteen pounds for a corpse! . . .

They move out of the Market, through the alleyways.

> NELLY. [In a harsh grumble as she trundles the barrow on with its load of rags and one cackling man.] Why don't you dig one up yourself? You 're frightened of the dark..

Over the cobbles of lonely alleys the barrow rattles, and the finger-snapping, dog-haired man squatting on the rags points his finger at one dark doorway, then at another.

> BROOM. They 're dead in there. . . . Dig 'em up, Fallon. . . . In there. . . . In there. . . .

Round a corner they come into Rag-and-Bone Alley.

24

RAG-AND-BONE ALLEY.

They stop at the door of a tenement.
In a first-floor window hangs a sign:

> CLEAN BEDS

Kate opens the door and goes through. Fallon follows her. Broom leaps from the barrow and is inside the dark doorway like a weasel into a hole.

LARGE LODGING-ROOM.

The four of them are moving through the room.

Around the walls of the room are many narrow beds.

Some of these beds are occupied. By men, or by women, or by human beings at all, we cannot see, but we can hear the noises of unhappy sleep, the sodden snore, the broken sigh, the whimpering of breath.

The four move through the room towards a small open door.

The two women go through the door into the darkness of the adjoining room.

Fallon stops at the last two beds against the wall. He looks down upon them.

In each of them sleeps an old man covered with rags.

One old man is mumbling in his sleep the almost inaudible scraps and ends of prayer.

And as Fallon looks down upon him, Broom tiptoes to his side.

Silently Fallon and Broom look down upon the two old sleeping men, whose hideously haggard faces for a moment we see close.

26

LECTURE HALL OF ROCK'S ACADEMY.

CLOSE-UP of Rock lecturing. He has a large volume in his hand.

> ROCK. This, gentlemen, is a volume by Vesalius, the acknowledged father of our art. Look at its size, and bear in mind that its thousand folio pages . . .

From Rock's angle we look down at the densely packed auditorium of his Lecture Hall. Among the faces of the students we recognize those of Brown and Harding.

> ROCK. [Continuing throughout.] . . . embrace only a special part of the human anatomy. . . . Now, gentlemen . . .

From the auditorium we look up at Rock as, with a very small volume in his other hand, he continues:

> ROCK. . . . behold the advance of the age, the progress of science to-day, the *Pocket Anatomist,* said to contain the *whole* of Anatomy within the compass of three inches by two.

Reverently he lays down the large volume on his lecturing table.
With the greatest contempt he casts the small volume across the platform.
Laughter of the students.

27

PRIVATE SMOKEROOM IN AN INN.

A snug little box of a room that could not hold more than four.
Two small oak settles facing each other.
A fire-place. A blazing wood fire.
A mantelpiece. A shining ebony clock. On either side of the clock, a tall silver candlestick. Candles burning.
A little counter. Behind the counter, bottles gleaming in candle-light.
Two old gentlemen are seated in the room. They have an air of judicious, contented permanency. They seem part of the furniture; their baldness gleams like the silver, like the mellow bottles. Each holds a silver tankard.

> FIRST GENTLEMAN. Now if I had a boy . . .
>
> SECOND GENTLEMAN. . . . He'd be no boy now, John . . .
>
> FIRST GENTLEMAN. . . . If I had a boy and he decided to enter the medical profession—against my wishes, needless to say; the legal profession has always been good enough for us—I would no more send him to Thomas Rock than I'd lay down the law to my wife. Your health!
>
> SECOND GENTLEMAN. Health!
>
> FIRST GENTLEMAN. They tell me, for example, that he openly condones the activities of the Resurrectionists. . . .

SECOND GENTLEMAN. He married a young person who was in domestic employment, too, I believe. . . .

FIRST GENTLEMAN. No, Richard, my wife tells me that she sold fish. . . .

SECOND GENTLEMAN. It is all the same—fish or dish-clouts.

FIRST GENTLEMAN. And I have heard that he has a most scurrilous tongue. . . . Preaches Anarchy. . . . Ridicules the Law. . . . Has all his young men *laughing*, and spouting revolutionary doctrine. . . . Interpolates violent criticisms of the Constitution in the very middle of his supposedly scientific lectures. . . . He does not even try to live like a gentleman. . . . My wife says that they keep only *one* maid in the whole house. . . .

SECOND GENTLEMAN. Mrs. Rock can do the rest of the work, I suppose. She is used to it.

FIRST GENTLEMAN. No, no, Richard, she sold fish. . . .

SECOND GENTLEMAN. Another, John?

FIRST GENTLEMAN. Thank you. . . . No more than a double. . . .

The First Gentleman raises his hand in a restraining gesture.

DISSOLVE to

28

Bright sunshine.

Students rushing pell-mell across THE SQUARE towards Rock's Academy.

A baker, carrying a big wooden tray of loaves across the Square, only just manages to avoid them.

We see the students race up the steps.

29

We see the students in the LECTURE HALL OF ROCK'S ACADEMY.

Rock enters.

He enters like a great actor; he acknowledges the ovation of his audience; he bows; he steps to the platform table; he adjusts his spectacles and his cuffs; every movement is studied.

    ROCK. Gentlemen . . .

DISSOLVE to

30

LECTURE HALL AT NIGHT.

The hall is dimly lit.

Rock, in shirt-sleeves, is rehearsing a lecture to an audience of one solitary skeleton.

> ROCK. . . . And are we to be told that the Kafir is a savage because he lives in the wilds, and that John Bull is the happy creature of civilization because he wears breeches, learns catechism, and cheats his neighbours? I say that . . .

During this rehearsal, the door of the Lecture Hall opens slowly, and two very young students poke their heads around to watch the master in uncomprehension and awe.

31

CLOSE-UP of two elderly professors, in mortar-boards and gowns, standing against the background of a very large, ornately gold-framed portrait of another old professor.

> FIRST PROFESSOR. I knew him when he was a boy. He was clever as a monkey, and he looked like one, too. But he was never *really young*.
>
> SECOND PROFESSOR. Or sound.
>
> FIRST PROFESSOR. No, one cannot say one likes him, or approves of him. But that is not the question. We must disregard personal prejudice.
>
> SECOND PROFESSOR. Difficult, when *he* refuses to disregard it. He called me 'insipid booby' in the *Scientific Journal*. . . .

FIRST PROFESSOR. [With a side glance at his companion.] Most uncalled for. No, my point is that one cannot look upon him as an insignificant opponent. His medical history is, unfortunately, brilliant. And they *do* think very highly of him on the Continent. Add to that, that he has five hundred students attending his classes, and that his nearest rival, our old friend Hocking, has less than a dozen. . . .

SECOND PROFESSOR. Nine, to be exact, and that includes three nephews. . . .

FIRST PROFESSOR. . . . and we begin to see what a pernicious influence the fellow might have upon the whole scholastic life of the City; indeed, upon the trend of scholastic thought *everywhere*. . . .

SECOND PROFESSOR. A menace. A menace. So rude, too. . . .

32

ROCK LECTURING.

He holds a human skull high in his hands.

33

CLOSE SHOT, from above, of an Old Man lying in his coffin.

We recognize him as one of the two old men who were sleeping when Fallon and Broom looked down at them in Sequence 25.

The lid of the coffin comes down.

TRACK BACK to show that we are in the Large Lodging-room of Fallon and Broom's house.

A Coffin Carpenter is nailing the coffin which lies at the foot of a bed. The straw of the bed lies scattered round it.

In the next bed, the other Old Man, wrapped in his rags, is staring at the coffin, at the Carpenter, and at Fallon and Broom, who stand at the entrance to the small adjoining room.

The rest of the beds in the Lodging-room are empty.

> BROOM. Hammer him in, hammer him in. Four pounds rent all dead in a box.
>
> FALLON. Now who would 've thought old Daniel could be so mean. Dying without a word, and owing us four pounds. He didn't even have a penny piece hidden under the straw. . . .
>
> BROOM. If only he was alive again so that I could kill him with my hands. . . .
>
> FALLON. And all he left was a bit of a broken pipe. . . .
>   And livin' here all these months on the fat of the land. . . . Many 's the night I 've beaten the rats off him my-self. . . .

Fallon is slouched against the doorway in a kind of self-pitying gloom, but Broom is half dancing with rage. . . .

The Carpenter goes on hammering.

> BROOM. Four pounds gone! Whisky and gin and bonnets gone! No more money for Broom! Hammer him in— hammer him in!
>
> COFFIN CARPENTER. [Without looking up.] And what do you think I 'm doing? Pullin' him out?

The beating of the hammer on the nails of the coffin.

And slowly Broom's dancing fury dies; he swivels his eyes towards Fallon.

Fallon looks back at him, and slowly through his mulish blood-shot stupidity he seems to understand.

Now the Carpenter rises, collects his tools, goes out through the far door.

> FALLON. [In a heavy whisper.] Hammer him in, hammer him in . . .
>
> BROOM. [Softly.] . . . and what do you think I 'm doing . . . [More loudly.] . . . pullin' him out?

Broom runs swiftly to the far door, looks out, turns back, slams the
door, bolts it, runs back. . . .

> BROOM. Four pounds he owes us and ten pounds they 'll give
> us for him. . . .
> FALLON. [With a kind of sodden horror.] Body-snatchers!

But Broom is calling through the other door:

> BROOM. Kate, Kate, come here!

Nelly and Kate come in.

> BROOM. Here, take one end. Take his head.

Without understanding, the women obey, take hold of the top of
the coffin while Broom takes the other. Together they drag the
coffin through the door into the other room. Still Fallon does
not move.
Then, suddenly, he draws back his heavy, muscle-bound shoulders,
and follows them.
And the eyes of the Old Man in the bed follow *him*.
We hear whispering from the other room.
Then a scraping, screwing noise.
Then the door is shut.

34

CITY STREET.

Late evening.

We see, in *LONG SHOT*, Fallon and Broom moving up the
street away from camera.
Fallon is carrying a tea-chest on his back.
By his side, at a zany trot, goes Broom.
We see two policemen coming slowly down the street towards them
and towards us.
And Fallon and Broom move quickly and suddenly down a side
street.

35

ANOTHER CITY STREET.

Late evening.

Fallon and Broom walking along with the tea-chest.

Two students pass them.

Broom nudges Fallon, who puts down the tea-chest and follows them a few steps.

> FALLON. [In his whining voice.] Beg your pardon me askin', sirs, if it's not too much trouble for you, could you be telling me where the Academy is? We've a little matter of business . . .

The students have paused and turned round.

> FIRST STUDENT. What Academy do you want?
> SECOND STUDENT. . . . And what's the little business? Oh!

The Second Student has seen the tea-chest a little way off, with Broom, its attendant, winking and leering.

He draws the First Student's attention to the tea-chest.

> FIRST STUDENT. If it's a subject . . .

Fallon cringes, and nods, and nods again.

> FIRST STUDENT. . . . take it along to Doctor Rock's. That's over there. Round that corner. It's the second house in the square. He'll pay you a better price than Hocking.
> FALLON. Oh yes, that was the name, sirs, Hocking, sirs, Hocking. . . .
> FIRST STUDENT. You take it to Doctor Rock. . . .
> FALLON. Oh, thank you, sirs, thank you, my humblest thanks to you, sirs. . . .

But the two students have walked off.

And Fallon rejoins the tea-chest and Broom, and lifts the tea-chest on his back and moves on. . . .

36

Broom raps at the door, then quickly steps back, ready to run.

Fallon, with the tea-chest, stands, bowed, near the door, stubbornly servile.

The grille in the door opens, and the face of Tom stares through: a face through a spider-web.

Through the grille, through Tom's eyes, we see the two men: the barrel-bulk of Fallon in the foreground, the lean lank Broom craning a little way behind him.

> FALLON. [Ingratiatingly.] Two young gentlemen told us we could sell an article here. . . . We got it in the tea-chest. . . .

Now, from Fallon's eyes, we see the face of Tom at the grille.

> TOM. [With a grunt.] Wait.

The grille closes. Bolts rattle. The door opens slowly.

We hear Tom's voice from the darkness within the door, but we do not see him.

> TOM'S VOICE. Come in. Walk quiet.

From behind them we see Fallon and Broom walk into the darkness. The door closes.

37

HALLWAY OF ROCK'S ACADEMY.

In the gloom, what stands within the tall, glass-fronted cases that line the Hallway cannot clearly be seen. But Fallon and Broom glance quickly, fearfully, at them, and we catch for a moment the glint of a bone, the shape of a stripped head.

Tom beckons, and walks down the Hall towards the door under the stairs.

> TOM. Follow. Walk quiet.

Fallon and Broom follow him into the small, dark, bare Cloak-room.

>TOM. Put it down there. Wait. Don't move now.

Tom goes out, leaving Fallon and Broom standing one at each side of the tea-chest in the dark room.

Tom walks into the Hall, climbs the stairs.

38

CORRIDOR IN ROCK'S ACADEMY.

Tom walks along the Corridor. He stops at a door.

From within we hear the voice of Rock:

>ROCK'S VOICE. . . . It was Herophilus who first traced the arachnoid membrane into the ventricles of the brain and . . .

Tom knocks three times on the door, and we hear Rock interrupt his sentence to say:

>ROCK'S VOICE. Come in.

And Tom enters.

From the open door we see into:

39

REFERENCE LIBRARY IN ROCK'S ACADEMY.

It is a smallish book-lined room, in which Rock is talking, in-formally, to a small group of seated students. He is walking up and down before them, his arms behind his back, but he stops at sight of Tom and raises his eyebrows questioningly.

>TOM. [In a confidential voice.] There's a couple of new hands downstairs, sir, they've brought . . .

But Rock, turning to the students, interrupts him.

>ROCK. Excuse me, gentlemen, you and Herophilus must wait a few moments.

And he walks out of the room, Tom stepping back to allow him
  passage.
Then Tom follows him.

40

CORRIDOR IN ROCK'S ACADEMY.

We follow Rock and Tom along the Corridor, down the stairs, and
  into the Hallway.
They go into the Cloak-room under the stairs.

41

SMALL CLOAK-ROOM.

Fallon and Broom move aside nervously into the shadows as Rock,
  taking no notice of them at all, goes straight to the tea-chest.
Tom hurries to his side, cuts the ropes around the chest, drags away
  the straw and rags.
Rock looks inside.
Then he straightens up, takes out a purse, hands it to Tom.

      ROCK. Give them seven pounds ten.

As Tom opens the purse and counts out the money from it, Rock,
  for the first time, looks at Fallon and Broom.

      ROCK. What are your names?

Fallon steps, toadying, out of the shadows.

      FALLON. Bob Fallon, sir.

Rock nods towards the shadows.

      ROCK. And the other?

Broom comes out, like a ghost, smiling his long side smile, but he
  does not speak. His long fingers rap-rap-rap on his elbow.

      FALLON. Broom, sir.

      ROCK. If you have any more, let us have them.

Rock turns away and walks out of the room. And Tom hands
  over the money to Fallon.

42

CITY SQUARE.

Music.

Fallon and Broom are moving through the moonlit Square towards us, Rock's Academy behind them.

Broom is half dancing, finger-snapping, his whole body one long lean grin.

Fallon, at his side clinking coins in his hand, is shambling an accompanying dance.

Nearer, nearer, they dance towards us until their faces fill the screen; until all we can see is the thick snout-mouth and the thin fox-lips, the little glinting eyes and the slant slits.

43

INTERIOR OF TAVERN B.

Closely we see, at a table, the faces of Fallon, Broom, Nelly, and Kate.

Coming closer, at the level of the table, we move past mugs and bottle to a pile of coins and Fallon's hands around them. The hands move, pushing some of the coins across the table.

> FALLON'S VOICE. For you, Nelly love. All for yourself. For you, Kate.

Now, still closely, we see the four at the table.

> FALLON. Broom and I share the rest.

And Fallon divides, in one movement of his broad fingers like big toes, the remaining coins.
Broom snatches his coins up.

> BROOM. A bottle, a bottle, another bottle!

And he darts away from the table and brings a bottle back and pours whisky into each mug.

NELLY. [Softly, in a kind of drunken, lumpish amazement.]
Seven pounds ten for an *old* man. . . .

And they all drink.

FALLON. Oh, the shame that he wasn't a *young* man. . . .

And, with their own kinds of laughter, they drink again.

44

MARKET-PLACE.

Day.

Fallon and Broom are looking at the wares on a clothes-stall.
They plough and scatter through the clothes, while the stall-keeper,
a fat woman smoking a pipe, looks on expressionlessly.
Fallon pulls out a shawl from a heap of oddments and tosses a coin
to the woman who, still expressionlessly but with the deftness of a
trained seal, catches it.

FALLON. I 'll have this . . .

He pulls out another shawl, and a skirt, and a petticoat.

FALLON. . . . and this . . . and this . . . and this . . .

And Broom has decked himself with lace from the stall and is
mincing around in the parody of a drunken woman.
Fallon, with a wide, extravagant gesture, piles all his presents under
his arm, and tosses the woman another coin. She catches it.
And Broom still prances, now with a bonnet on his head.

BROOM. Look at me. . . . look at me. My *mother* wouldn't
know me. . . .

And Fallon and Broom link arms and move away through the
Market, Broom in his fineries, Fallon trailing a shawl behind him
in the mud of the cobbles.
Arm in arm they move on through the Market, to the distant playing
of a fiddle.

44

45

Music.

A windy afternoon.

Rock and Elizabeth are walking down a path under the trees. Annabella walks a little way apart from them, stiffly, primly.

Some way in front of them two little children are running along and playing.

Through the music we hear the voice of Rock's mind.

> ROCK'S VOICE. Oh, such a cold day for walking abroad, and the wind like a drunk beggar with his fiddle. Well, I suppose it does us good. It does *me* good to feel the family man again, walking through the respectable, gusty park with Elizabeth on my arm. . . . Oh, the years fly! Time with his wingèd chariot, hurrying near, and my life going true and even, and my children growing, and Elizabeth with me for ever, and books to write, and work to do. . . . Lord, but it's a happy time . . . even in the unhappy times. . . .

Slowly, sedately, they move on through the cold afternoon.

46

RAG-AND-BONE ALLEY.

Slowly, disconsolately, Fallon and Broom walk down the Alley towards the Lodging-house.

Broom is no longer dancing, finger-snapping, pirouetting, but walks like a wraith, holding his shabby thinness against the cold; and Fallon, head down, shambles without seeing or caring.

They reach the Lodging-house.

47

LARGE LODGING-ROOM.

All the beds are empty, the earth-coloured blankets flung half off them.

All the beds except one: that bed nearest to the door of the small adjoining room, in which the second Old Man lies still under his filth and rags.

Fallon and Broom walk past the Old Man, open the door of the small room.

His eyes follow them.

The door closes.

48

SMALL ROOM IN LODGING-HOUSE.

In one corner a straw bed.

In another, heaps of rags.

There is a table, a few broken chairs.

Straw and broken glass litter the foul floor.

Fallon throws himself on to the straw bed.

Broom walks about the room, caged, his eyes darting sharply at every squalor.

> FALLON. And what d' you think you 'll find? Prowling like a cat. D' you think there 's money in the old straw?

Broom has stopped at the cobwebbed window and is looking out.

> BROOM. There 's fat pigs in the yard outside.
>
> FALLON. [Not listening.] Drain the dry bottles, lick the floor, scrabble in the muck for a farthing. There 's nothing, nothing.
>
> BROOM. [Still at the window.] Fat, juicy porkers waiting for the knife to cut them ear to ear. Squeeeel!
>
> FALLON. Shut your squeal. Ach, if old Daniel was here, dying again!
>
> BROOM. [In a quiet voice, still looking out of the window.] Geordie 's dying.

Without turning from the window, Broom nods back at the door
between the small room and the large room.
We move towards Broom.

> BROOM. Geordie coughs all night. Krawf! Krawf!

We move closer to Broom.

> BROOM. [Softly, but clearly.] It's awful *tedious* waiting for
> Geordie to die. . . .

We are right up to Broom's face.
There is complete silence.
Then there is the sound of the rustle of straw. Then the sound of
a door opening
Still Broom does not look round.
Only when a cry comes from the next room, a cry like an old sheep's,
half moan and half bleat, does Broom spin round like a dancer at a cue.
We see him, in CLOSE-UP, staring towards the other room.
Staring. And smiling.

DISSOLVE.

49

CITY STREET.

Music.

Late evening.

LONG SHOT of Fallon and Broom walking away from camera.
Fallon carries the tea-chest on his back.
Broom capers at his side.

50

LARGE LODGING-ROOM.

Kate and Nelly walking through the room.
They stop at the Old Man's bed.
Nelly leans down to look at the empty bed. Then she straightens
up with a little shudder.

And Kate looks.

Silently they pull up the rags and bits of blanket from where they have been pulled on to the floor, and cover the straw bed with them, carefully, like two housewives.

Suddenly, from outside, there is a loud knocking on the door.

The women start, look at each other.

> NELLY. [Whispering.] Perhaps that's the . . .
> KATE. [Whispering.] Perhaps it's . . . lodgers.

And straightening her dirty shawls about her, she walks down the room to see.

51

HALLWAY OF ROCK'S ACADEMY.

Tom is climbing the stairs. From the foot of the stairs we see him climb.

He is half-way up when Rock, with top-hat and stick, comes down.

Tom stops.

As Rock approaches him, Tom speaks:

> TOM. It's Bob Fallon and Broom again, sir. They've brought a new subject. It's an old man. He's not . . . very long dead. They want ten pounds, sir.
> ROCK. Give it to them.

He walks downstairs, down towards us. His face is expressionless, his attire immaculate.

52

CITY CHURCH.

Organ music as the worshippers come out into the street.

Among the worshippers, distinguished by his loose-flowing cloak and his florid clothing, is Rock.

With him are four of his students, including Brown whom last we saw in Tavern B with Murray and Jennie Bailey. Other of the faces we recognize, too, as having been among those in the lecture classes.

Many of the worshippers stop outside the church, bow, raise their hats, gather in groups.

But Rock and his four disciples stride on down the street.

From outside the church we see how the eyes of many worshippers follow them; and a few black-apparelled heads come whispering together.

The organ music fades.

53

HILL ABOVE THE CITY.

Rock and the students are walking up the Hill.
They stop. They look down at the City.
Rock sits on the grass, and the students sit at his feet.

> BROWN. Did you ever hear such a mealy-mouthed sermon, sir? It made me . . .
>
> ROCK. Indeed? In my student days I fancied myself as something of a sermon-taster, but I cannot say that I was ever actually ill from it. I grew accustomed to the taste: a not too unpleasant mixture of boiled brimstone and the day before yesterday's sprouts. . . .
>
> FIRST STUDENT. What was the sermon about? The Sanctity of Human Life, was it? I went to sleep.
>
> ROCK. To sleep, Mr. Duncan? I would not have known. You seemed to me to be wearing the same expression of studious concentration that you wear in my Anatomy classes. How strange and beautiful the City looks to-day. A city where good men walk in dignity and peace, and children play in green places, and girls are both pure and merry, and the hearts of young men are lifted with the aspirations of love, and scholars labour diligently with no other motive

49

than the advancement of the knowledge and happiness of mankind. Dear me! Who would think that that lovely City below us is a Gibraltar of propriety and mediocrity, where the good men starve or are hounded into the dark, and the worthless thrive, and the scholars think only of material rewards, and the girls are born with their noses snobbed in the air and their eyes searching for a marriage bargain, and the young men's hearts are lifted only by the thought of easy success. And who would think, too, that within that Gibraltar lies an *inner* island of active evil. . . .

BENNET. [Slowly.] Yes. The Sanctity of the Human Body and the Human Soul. That's what the sermon was about, sir. It's my opinion that . . .

ROCK. Ah! An opinion! Gentlemen, what priceless treasure is to be revealed to us now. . . .

BENNET. [Blushing, and very confused.] I was only going to say, sir, that I haven't got much of an opinion about it anyway. . . .

ROCK. [To the others.] What did I tell you? A treasure! 'My opinion is that I have no opinion.' Excellent! . . . But let us talk about other things. . . .

That Rabelaisian *raconteur*, Mr. Bennet, shall tell us some disreputable stories of his early youth.

And the very young Mr. Bennet is confused again.

DISSOLVE to

Rock and students walking downhill.
Music.
Gathering darkness.
At the foot of the hill, Brown and Students One and Two part from Rock and Bennet.
We see them in *LONG SHOT.*
We hear none of their words, but only the evening music.

CUT to

54

Music.

Darkness gathering deeper.

The lights are coming on. Lights in the windows of the taverns, and tallow-sticks flaring at the alley corners and outside a few of the Market houses.

But the ordinary life of the Market does not cease with the dark and the coming on of the lights. Children still play on the cobbies; and from the alleys behind them, in the unseen courts and closes, come the voices of other children. And men and women stand about in shop and house and tavern doorways, drinking, talking, quarrelling. And a horse and cart rumble out of darkness, over the cobbles, and into darkness again.

We see Rock and Bennet walking through the Market, towards us.

And we see, too, the crippled boy with the idiot smile (whom we first saw in Sequence 2) playing among a little crowd of children.

He runs away from the children, over to Rock.

And Rock stops, and smiles at him.

> ROCK. Good evening, Billy.

Billy smiles back delightedly, and bobs his head up and down.

> ROCK. It's a cold night to be running about in the streets. . . .
> BILLY. Not for Billy Bedlam. . . . Not cold. . . . [And, like a taught parrot, he gabbles.] He's never cold in September or November or December. . . .
> ROCK. [Patiently.] Why, Billy?
> BILLY. Because there's an ember in the month. . . .

Rock puts money gently into Billy's hand.

> ROCK. Here's a present for you, boy. Hold it in your hand. Don't lose it.

Rock and Bennet walk on.

We hear, from behind them, Billy's voice crying:

    BILLY'S VOICE. Night . . . night . . . Doctor Rock. . . .

And we move with Rock and Bennet through the night-time Market.

    ROCK. Now he'll hurry as fast as he can on his bent bones to the nearest tavern, and fuddle his few poor wits, and crack his crazed little jokes half remembered from the cradle. . . . Oh, how the pious would lift their hands to heaven to think of a man giving money to an idiot so that he could get drunk and be warm and happy for an hour or two. Let him rather die a sober frozen idiot in the gutter! . . . Would you care to join me at dinner, sir? . . .

    BENNET. Thank you, Doctor. . . .

    ROCK. Don't call me Doctor. Do I call you Student? Come on, sir. . . .

And they walk out of the Market into:

55

ALLEYWAY.

Rock and Bennet walk on down the Alley, away from us, into darkness.

And we *TRACK UP* the Alley towards a doorway with a tallow-stick burning above it.

Two figures stand in the doorway: a man and a woman.

And coming closer to them, we see that they are Murray and Jennie Bailey.

They are very close together.

They stand, their faces half illuminated and half shadowed by the burning tallow-stick, as though in a little island surrounded by a sea of darkness.

And from that sea come the cries of children at play in the dark; though far off now.

    JENNIE. It's good night. . . . good night at the door again. Parting like strangers. . . .

MURRAY. You 're close to me for a moment. . . .

JENNIE. Is a moment enough for you, then, my dear, my dear? And all the long night to go. . . . You 're a sad, strange boy, saying you love me and leaving me all alone. . . .

MURRAY. It 's I 'll be all alone. . . .

JENNIE. Draw a pretty picture of me, then, to carry about with you so that you 'll never be alone, and put it under your pillow at nights like a girl puts a lock of hair or a bit of weddin' cake to wish her sweetheart will come to her. . . .

MURRAY. I couldn't draw *your* picture, Jennie. You 're never the same for a single minute. [Softly.] But you 're always beautiful. I *know* you now; but sometimes I don't know you at all—when you 're gay and *hard* and drinking and dancing. . . . And not caring. . . . It 's the others that know you then. . . .

JENNIE. Oh, my sweet, you and your silly—others. . . . Come inside with me now. . . .

And Jennie opens the dark door beneath the burning tallow-stick.

And we see a little passage-way, lit by a gas-jet. And a curtain at the end of the passage-way.

And from behind the curtain we hear the voices of men and women.

Jennie stands against the passage light, with the other light bright about her head.

MURRAY. No. No, Jennie. Good night.

And he kisses her, and turns away quickly.

And she steps into the passage-way, and closes the door as the voices behind the curtain rise. . . .

56

DINING-ROOM OF ROCK'S HOUSE.

From the angle of the door we see that under the light of the high, many-branched candlesticks sit Rock, Bennet, Annabella, and Elizabeth.

We TRACK UP to the table.

They are drinking coffee, but there is a decanter at Rock's elbow. Annabella is frigidly angry.

ANNABELLA. . . . And that is what I *believe*, and that is what is right. . . .

ROCK. [Pointedly to Bennet.] Have some brandy. . . .

ANNABELLA. There can be, and there always has been, only *one* path of virtue.

ROCK. Surprisingly I agree with you, Annabella.

ANNABELLA. Then it is only for the second time in your life.

ROCK. I can't remember the first. But I agree with what you say, not with what you *mean*. *I believe in the virtue of following no path but your own, wherever it leads.* . . .

ANNABELLA. And that is precisely the sort of statement that antagonizes you to the whole of the profession. . . .

For all your great successes and your famous friends, you do not know how many people there are who would be delighted to see you ruined. . . .

ELIZABETH. [To Bennet.] Do you like this City, Mr. Bennet, after the Continent? I think you were very fortunate to have travelled around so much with your parents in the holidays. . . .

BENNET. I like France, ma'am, very much indeed. Of course, I like this City, too. . . .

ANNABELLA. Mr. Bennet, do you, as a student, find that my brother's language and attitude are congenial to the other students?

ROCK. How d' you find the brandy, Bennet? Not mellow enough for you?

BENNET. No, sir . . . it's . . . excellent. Yes, Miss Rock, we all find Doctor Rock's language and . . . er . . . attitude . . . most . . . congenial and, and . . . and *stimulating.*

ANNABELLA. Like brandy on persons of weak health, physical or mental.

ELIZABETH. I should very much like to see Paris, Mr. Bennet. . . .

ANNABELLA. My dear Elizabeth, is this a geographical con-versazione? I merely wanted to know . . .

ROCK. [To Bennet.] Without embarrassing you further, and allowing you no opportunity of savouring, let alone swallowing, the brandy you were kind enough to call excellent, may I explain to you that what my sister really wishes to know is whether you agree with her that the medical profession, with some notable exceptions, consider me a seducer of youth and an atheist? [In another tone.] You have no need to answer, of course. . . . [Gently.] Has he, Elizabeth, my dear? I would far prefer to talk about Paris. . . .

BENNET. [In an agony of embarrassment, but still determined to defend his master.] I can't pretend to know what the medical profession thinks of Doctor Rock, Miss Rock, but *we* all think that most of the other doctors and professors are enormously *jealous* of him. [To Elizabeth.] Jealous be-cause he's a great anatomist, ma'am, and a great—— [He breaks off.]

ROCK. H'm! I know Paris well, especially the cafés. I always used to wear a yachting cap in France, I can't think why. . . . I wish you'd been there with me, my dear. . . .

DISSOLVE to

57

SMALL ROOM IN LODGING-HOUSE.

Nelly, at the fire, is stirring a wooden spoon in a black pot, and something is being fried. We hear the sizzling.

Kate, with an almost bristleless broom, is brushing the broken glass into a corner.

The broken table has been laid: there are four pewter mugs on it.

Suddenly there is a noise of singing and stamping from outside.

The door is crashed open and Broom dances in, a bottle under each arm.

He winks and leers at the women, nods and jerks his fingers at the open door.

And in through the door Fallon staggers, singing, with a little old woman hanging, half falling, on his arm. She too is trying to sing.

> FALLON. And look what I've brought home, my doves. A pretty old woman with nowhere to sleep . . . have you, Granny? Nowhere to sleep but with us. Shall we give her a bed?
>
> NELLY. Where d'you find her?

Broom is opening a bottle and pouring whisky into the mugs. He gives the Old Woman one.

> BROOM. Drink with Broom!
>
> FALLON. She was lying in the gutter like an old cabbage, weren't you, Granny? Her poor grey hairs dragging in the mud. And who should pick her up but kind Bob?

Fallon lifts the Old Woman up and places her on the bed.

> FALLON. There. The place of honour. Nothing's too good for her.
>
> KATE. What you're going to do?
>
> BROOM. Do? Drink!
>
> FALLON. Do? Drink with Granny. All night long.

The Old Woman titters and drinks. She nearly falls off the bed, but Fallon catches her and lays her down gently.

> FALLON. [Softly.] No harm must come to you now. You might have bumped your head. Then what'd the doctors think?

Broom skips over and takes the Old Woman's mug from her hand and pours whisky down her throat.

She coughs and gasps.

> FALLON. [In a different voice, to the women.] You two be running off on an errand.

Broom points at the Old Woman who is now almost unconscious, spread on her back, her black mouth open.

BROOM. You needn't be long.

FALLON. [Slowly.] Go now.

And the women, without a word, and without looking at the Old
Woman, fasten their shawls and go out.

FALLON. [To the Old Woman, as though to a child.]   Up
you get, dear.   Don't you want no more whisky?   [Into
her ear.]   Whisky, whisky!

And, trembling, the Old Woman manages to regain some conscious-
ness.   As soon as she does, Broom, ready all the time, pours more
whisky down her throat.
She falls back.

FALLON. Give me the bottle.

Broom hands it to him.   Fallon drinks from it.   He passes the bottle
back.   He rubs off the sweat from his forehead.   He moves,
unsteadily, but heavily, to the head of the bed.
And Broom crouches at the foot.
From above, we look down on to the Old Woman's face.
Her eyes open.
Suddenly her face is frightened.

58

CITY SQUARE.

We see Fallon and Broom through the grille in the door of Rock's
Academy, as through prison bars.
Fallon carries the tea-chest.
Now, from behind Fallon and Broom, we see the door opened by
Tom.
We follow Fallon and Broom as they enter the Hallway.

59

HALLWAY OF ROCK'S ACADEMY.

Without any need for instruction from Tom, Fallon and Broom
move with the tea-chest into the Cloak-room under the stairs.

As they go in, so Murray, in evening dress, comes down the stairs
and sees them.

In the Hallway he beckons Tom over to him.

>MURRAY. Who are the dapper gentlemen?

>TOM. Bob Fallon and Broom, sir. They're new hands . . .
>but they're getting pretty regular. They ask for ten pounds.

Murray goes into the Cloak-room and comes out a moment later.
He nods his head.

>MURRAY. That'll do.

Now, from the back of the Hallway, at the foot of the stairs, we see
Tom opening the door wide to Murray.

In the street outside we see a stationary coach.

>MURRAY. [At the door.] If any more bodies call, tell them
>I'm at the theatre with Doctor Rock. Good evening, Tom.

And we see him, in *LONG SHOT* from the back of the Hallway,
walk out, down the steps, and into the coach.

60

VESTIBULE OF THEATRE.

At the door leans Jennie Bailey, with a gay shawl round her shoulders.

We see, outside the Theatre, coaches waiting.

There is a great burst of applause, and she turns round to look
towards the door of the auditorium.

The audience pours out.

Down the stairs at the side come Rock, Elizabeth, Green, Murray,
and Annabella.

From Jennie's angle we see them stop to talk to other members of
the audience.

We see Murray looking round him.

We see Hocking.

TRACK UP close to Rock's party.

>HOCKING. Good evening, Doctor Rock.

>ROCK. Good evening, Doctor Hocking.

HOCKING. I do not often see you at the play . . .

ROCK. No, sir. I am able to find my entertainment else-
where. The City is full of low comedians: it is a pity that
the lowest of them all should also be a surgeon. Good night.

And Rock takes Elizabeth's arm, and leads his guests out.

The last of the party is Murray. He sees Jennie Bailey, and stops as
the others walk out to the waiting coaches.

He looks round him quickly, then whispers to her, and hurries
after the others.

Coaches drive off.

And Jennie goes out, too.

We follow her through the darkness until the Theatre lights behind
us fade.

DISSOLVE to

61

MARKET-PLACE.

Night.

We see the entrance to Tavern B from which light and voices pour
on to the cobbles.

Jennie Bailey comes out of darkness into the light and into the tavern.

62

INTERIOR OF TAVERN B.

The tavern is crowded.

Many of the faces are familiar to us now: That old bag of female
bones over there, she was the one who described to Fallon and
Broom the profession of Andrew Merry-Lees; that fat woman
with a pipe there, who tosses down her drink as a tamed seal
swallows a fish, she was the one who kept the stall where Fallon
and Broom bought clothes for their women; that humpback there,
looking at everything with an idiot smile, he is the one called
Billy Bedlam; one of those two very young men over there, being

wise and waggish to a pretty girl of sixteen, is the student Bennet;
that tall man in a scarecrow's top-hat, hiccuping solemnly, he is
the one called Andrew Merry-Lees; and there are others we have
seen before, in the tavern, in the street, in the Market, all of them,
in their way, vice-residents of the tavern; and among them a few
honest, very poor people.

We see all this through Jennie Bailey's eyes.

A dark, pretty young woman with a sulky expression, seated at the
far end of the room, waves her hand.

And from her view we see Jennie Bailey, in her gay shawl, charming
her way down the room, being familiar with every one (including
Billy Bedlam) and over-familiar with some.

Now we see that Jennie Bailey is sitting next to the dark young
woman.

And now we see them very close.

Jennie drinks from the dark girl's drink.

> JENNIE. I been to see the play in the theatre, Alice.
>
> ALICE. You didn't see no play, dear. You been up High
> Street.
>
> JENNIE. I did. From the outside. Who shall we get to
> buy us a drink?

She roves her eye round the pub. She nods towards Billy Bedlam.

> JENNIE. Him?

She nods towards Andrew Merry-Lees.

> JENNIE. Him? Oooh, no!

She nods towards Bennet. He catches her glance, is about to blush,
then, remembering his age, winks back.

> JENNIE. Him!

She smiles at Bennet, beckons him over. He comes over.

> JENNIE. Going to buy us some medicine, Doctor?
>
> BENNET. Oh, of course I am, Jennie. . . .
>
> JENNIE. Some for Alice and some for me? It's a cold night
> for poor working girls like us. . . .

Bennet goes off.

JENNIE. I saw my Doctor at the theatre. In my box.
ALICE. John Murray?

Jennie nods.

ALICE. Why d' you treat the poor creature so badly, Jennie?
JENNIE. Oh, but Alice darling, I'm so very very fond of
him. I like him better than any man in the whole world. . . .
ALICE. Then why d' you carry on in front of his eyes and . . .
JENNIE. Oh, but I don't, I don't. . . .
ALICE. . . . and teasing him that he's a parson's son, and
letting him see you walk out with any Tom, Dick, and
Harry. . . .
JENNIE. . . . I don't know any Harry. . . .
ALICE. . . . No one could know you loved him, you're so
brazen, dear. . . .
JENNIE. Oh, I want some fun before I die. . . . You're a
parson's daughter yourself. . . . He must love me for what
I am, that's all there is. . . .

Bennet comes back with two mugs.

JENNIE. There, you can always tell, he's got a sweet face.
. . . I *do* like students and doctors and . . .
ALICE. . . . butchers and bakers and candlestick-makers. . . .

We hear a high yelping laugh, and then Fallon's voice.

FALLON'S VOICE. And there's my darling Jennie. . . .
BROOM'S VOICE. And mine, and mine!

And Fallon and Broom stagger to the table, pushing Bennet aside.
Fallon pulls a bottle out of his pocket.

FALLON. Who's going to share a bottle with two county
gentlemen?

Fallon and Broom sit themselves next to Alice and Jennie, Fallon
next to Jennie, Broom to Alice. Fallon pulls two mugs across
the table, and fills them.

JENNIE. I never drink with strangers except on Mondays. . . .
FALLON. And it's *Monday* to-night.

O the stars are shining, the bells are chiming, we'll drink to Monday and Tuesday and . . .

Fallon pours out another drink.

> JENNIE. And I never drink twice with strangers before twelve o'clock. . . .
> FALLON. And Lord, it's *after twelve*.
>> O the moon is singing, the grass is growing. We'll drink to twelve o'clock . . . and one o'clock . . . and two o'clock. . . .

QUICK DISSOLVE to the same table with more mugs and bottles on it.

Fallon and Jennie are now very tipsy.

Broom is smiling, leering, giggling, and clowning to Jennie.

Alice still remains comparatively sober, and still sulky.

> FALLON. [Wheedling.] I got two more bottles in my little room, Miss Pretty Bailey. Two great bottles of dancin' dew that'll make you think the sun's shining in the middle of the night . . . and satiny shining couches for all the kings and queens to be lying on. . . . And . . .
> ALICE. We're not going.
> JENNIE. Will you give me a diamond ring and a golden bracelet and . . .
> FALLON. I'll give you a bucketful of pearls. We'll sing and dance. We'll be merry as crickets in Rag-and-Bone Alley. . . .
> JENNIE. [Half laughing, half singing.] We'll be merry as crickets in Rag-and-Bone Alley. . . .
> ALICE. [In an angry whisper to Jennie.] You're not going with these two creatures. . . . You must wait for John Murray. . . . Don't drink any more with that Bob Fallon. . . .
> BROOM. And I'll cook you liver and lights. . . .
> JENNIE. Will you cook a partridge for me? . . .
> FALLON. And I'll put a peacock's feathers in your hair. . . .
> JENNIE. Oh, listen to them both. . . . You'd think they

were great rich men with crowns and palaces, not a couple
of naughty tinkers. . . .

ALICE. We're not going. . . .

QUICK DISSOLVE to

63

MARKET-PLACE in the dim moonlight.

Four figures move through the Market: Fallon, Jennie, Broom, Alice.
Fallon and Jennie are singing.

FALLON AND JENNIE. We'll be merry as crickets in . . .
And Broom accompanies their singing, like a dog baying at the moon.
Now they are moving through:

64

RAG-AND-BONE ALLEY.

Their singing wakes up a shape that is lying in a dark doorway.
Slowly, awkwardly, it rises to its feet. It is Billy Bedlam.
He follows the four, with his eyes, down the Alley, and sees them
  enter the Lodging-house.

65

Darkness.

Fallon, Jennie, and Broom singing and baying in the darkness.
A door is flung open.
We see, for a moment, the small room of the Lodging-house.
  Nelly stands there at the dead fire.
Then Fallon and Jennie and Broom and Alice stumble into the
  light of the room.
Fallon lurches over to the table, opens a bottle with his teeth.
He makes an unsteady bow, offers the bottle to Jennie. . . .

FALLON. You first, my Jennie, my merry, my cricket. . . .
Jennie drinks.

Alice looks round the room with fear and revulsion.

Broom leaps on to the bed.

Nelly stands, drab and cross, before Fallon.

> NELLY. Who told you you could bring your women here,
> you and that mad dog. . . .
>
> FALLON. Now, now, Nelly macushla, we've come to sing
> and drink. . . .

But Nelly rushes across to Jennie and pulls the bottle from her lips.

> ALICE. [Urgently.] I told you not to come, Jennie Bailey.
> . . . Let's go, let's go!
>
> FALLON. My Jennie's not going, she's not going, any one
> else in the wide world can go, not Jennie.
>
> ALICE. Come on, Jennie, come on.

But Jennie is sitting, swinging her legs, on the table, and is trying
to open the other bottle.

> FALLON. If you don't like it here, go to your own pigsty.

Alice looks at Jennie, but Jennie has opened the bottle and is
pouring from it into a glass.

And Alice goes. She slams the door behind her.

> NELLY. And *she* goes, too.

Nelly, still with the one bottle in her hand, tries to tear the other
bottle from Jennie.

Fallon suddenly lifts a glass and throws it in Nelly's face.

As she staggers, he takes the bottle from her. She puts her hand up
slowly to her face, and feels the running blood.

And she goes out of the room like an old woman whipped.

Fallon takes Jennie's glass, drinks from it, puts it back in her hand.

And Jennie drinks, swinging her legs.

And Broom is dog-creeping on the floor. As Fallon and Jennie
drink he slips off the buckles from her shoes and leaps, lightly and
silently, to his feet, and is out of the room, closing the door with
no sound.

And Fallon's hand, as he looks at Jennie, slowly drops, and the drink
from the bottle he is holding runs over her dress and down her legs.

66

DOORWAY IN ALLEY (as in Sequence 55).

Alice is talking excitedly to a woman in the doorway.
The woman nearly fills the doorway. She is dressed in a long, loose
shift. Her huge arms are bare.

> ALICE. And I tried to tell her, Rosie, but she wouldn't
> listen, she was laughing and drinking with him. . . . Oh,
> I didn't like the looks of him, Rosie. . . .
> ROSIE. Go and fetch her back.

Rosie has a voice deep as a man's, and heavy, and slow.

> ALICE. But I'm telling you, Rosie, he's no good, he's like
> an *animal*; won't you send someone back with me? . . .
> ROSIE. Go and fetch her back. There's persons waiting for
> her here. . . .

Alice turns away.

67

Darkness.
The pattering of footsteps in the darkness.
A door is flung open.
We see into the small room of the Lodging-house.
But we see no one there.
Then Alice runs in, looks round. She sees Fallon lying stretched
on his back on the straw bed in the corner.

> ALICE. Where's Jennie?
> FALLON. [In a dulled voice.] Jennie? She went a long
> time ago.
> ALICE. Where did she go?
> FALLON. She went out.

And Alice runs out of the room, leaving the door open.

68

Alice is running down Rag-and-Bone Alley in the ·moonlight.
A dark shape leans against a doorway.
Alice stops.

> ALICE. Which way did Jennie go?

Billy Bedlam shakes his head.
Alice points up the Alley.

> ALICE. Did she go that way?

He shakes his head, and stretches out his hand.

> BILLY. Have some snuff. . . .

But Alice runs on up Rag-and-Bone Alley.

69

SMALL ROOM IN LODGING-HOUSE.

Fallon is still lying on the straw bed.
The door is still open.
Nelly comes in. The blood has dried on her cheek. She looks
round the room.

> NELLY. Where's Jennie?

He puts his hand down at his side, the side nearest the wall, and
drags up Jennie's gay shawl, and holds it up to Nelly.
His face is hot and wet.

FADE OUT.

FADE IN

70

CITY STREET.

Broad daylight.
Music and the ringing of church bells.
Fallon and Broom walking up street away from camera.

Fallon is carrying a sack on his back. Broom is holding the end of
the sack mock-solemnly like a man at the end of a coffin.

We see, as they move, children coming out of the doorways,
children scampering away from their play to sing and cry together:

> CHILDREN'S VOICES. You 've got a body in the sack!
> Body-snatchers!
> Dead!
> Dead!
> Dead!
> Body-snatchers!

And they dance around the sack.

And Broom snaps his teeth at them.

Fallon and Broom walk on. The voices fade behind them.

DISSOLVE to

71

CLOSE SHOT of the sack on a table.

TRACK BACK to see that the table is in the Dissecting Room of
Rock's Academy.

There are many students. Some, with their backs to us, are bent
over the tables, cutting, probing, snipping. We see their movements but not the objects upon which they are working. Some
of the students are talking together. None of them takes any
notice of the sack.

Murray comes in and walks up to the sack.

> MURRAY. [Casually.] Let 's see what we 've got to-day.

He begins to untie the thick ropes about the sack.

Several students gather around him.

> MURRAY. An old trull of eighty with bow legs and a belly
> like a Lord Mayor's, eh? A tramp from the gutter with
> cirrhosis of the liver and three teeth? What 's your guess?
> . . . An old . . .

He opens the neck of the sack, and begins to draw the sack down
from the head.

Suddenly he stops talking. We see what he sees: Jennie's long fair hair. Slowly he draws the sack down from the face, but we do not see it. The students, silent now, gather around it, and we see only their backs and the profile of Murray. We see that his face has hardened and become grim, his lips are held very tightly together, as though he were forcing himself not to utter a word.

> BENNET. [In a long-drawn-out half-sighing whisper.] God!
> FIRST STUDENT. Here, let me look.

The First Student bends closer over the table.

> FIRST STUDENT. It's Jennie Bailey.
> SECOND STUDENT. Sweet Jennie Bailey.
> BENNET. [Softly.] Yes, it's Jennie! I saw her last night in the Market. . . . She was *singing*. . . .

But Murray does not utter a word.

> THIRD STUDENT. How did she die? . . .
> BENNET. She was *singing* . . . and *dancing*. . . .

Suddenly Murray turns away and strides out of the room.
The students still stand around the body that we do not see.

72

Out in the HALLWAY Murray strides across to the door of the small Cloak-room.
The door is open. Beyond it is darkness. Murray calls into the darkness.

> MURRAY. Tom!

And from the darkness we hear Tom's voice:

> TOM'S VOICE. Coming, sir.

Tom comes out of the darkness like an underground animal. He blinks at the light.

> TOM. Yes, sir? I was . . . cleaning up.
> MURRAY. Who brought the subject in?
> TOM. In the sack, sir? That was Bob Fallon and Broom. . . . Wasn't it fresh, sir?

Murray turns away abruptly and, without a word, goes upstairs.
Now we see Murray walking along the Corridor.
He opens a door and strides in.

73

We see Murray stride into the REFERENCE LIBRARY.
Rock is standing at a bookshelf at the far end of the room, his back
to us and to Murray.
He turns round as Murray comes in.

> ROCK. You knock at the door very softly, Mr. Murray.

Murray closes the door, and stands with his back to it.
Rock stands with *his* back to the bookcase.   Murray speaks slowly,
deliberately, like a man with a passionate temper who is afraid to
lose control of it.

> MURRAY. They've got Jennie Bailey downstairs.
>
> ROCK. Indeed?   Jennie Bailey?   Oh yes, I think I remember
> the name.   A beautiful slut with a bold eye and a tongue
> like a drunken horse-thief's.
>
>   And what might she be doing downstairs?   I am sure,
> Mr. Murray, that she is an expert in Anatomy, but her
> knowledge would be too specialized. . . .   Or has she come
> merely to entertain?
>
> MURRAY. She has come, sir, to be dissected.
>
> ROCK. How very generous of her.   I did not think that
> science was so near her heart.   Does she wish to be dissected
> *alive*?
>
> MURRAY. She is dead.
>
> ROCK. That is carrying scientific generosity to its furthest
> limit.
>
> MURRAY. She was murdered.
>
> ROCK. [Sharply.] Who says so?
>
> MURRAY. She was murdered.
>
> ROCK. Are there signs of violence upon the body?

MURRAY. She was murdered by two paid thugs of yours: Fallon and Broom. I saw her last night after the theatre. She was well and gay. There are no signs of violence upon her body.

ROCK. Thugs of *mine*, Mr. Murray? Do you remember that you yourself paid them for the last *three* subjects?

MURRAY. She was murdered. I saw her. [Slowly, rememberingly.] She had a red shawl on.

ROCK. Indisputable evidence that she was murdered. She should have worn a white shawl, for purity. And what if she *was* murdered, Mr. Murray? We are anatomists, not policemen; we are scientists, not moralists. Do *I, I,* care if every lewd and sottish woman of the streets has her throat slit from ear to ear? She served no purpose in life save the cheapening of physical passion and the petty traffics of lust. Let her serve her purpose in death.

MURRAY. You hired Fallon and Broom to murder her as you hired them to murder the others.

ROCK. I need bodies. They brought bodies. I pay for what I need. I do not hire murderers. . . .

Rock walks over to the door. Murray still has his back to it. Rock stops. Their eyes meet. Then Murray moves aside. Rock opens the door and walks out. We see him walking down the Corridor.

74

CUT. DISSECTING ROOM OF ROCK'S ACADEMY.

Rock walks in.

Students are gathered round the table where Jennie's body lies. We do not see the body.

The students move aside as Rock enters.

He stands in the middle of the group. For a moment he is silent, his head held a little to one side, looking down at the unseen body.

Then Rock turns away from the table.
Murray stands at the door.

> Rock. Oh, Mr. Murray. I think that before the body is
> put into the brine bath, a drawing should be made of it.
> Shall we not allow posterity to share our exhilaration at the
> sight of such perfect physical beauty?
>
> I should be much obliged if you yourself would perpetuate
> on paper the loveliness of this poor clay, Mr. Murray. We
> know your skill with the pencil. God should have made
> you an artist. He did the next best thing: he gave you a
> very vivid imagination.

And Rock walks out of the Dissecting Room.
Murray does not move.
The eyes of the students are upon him.

75

A CITY STREET IN THE FASHIONABLE AREA.

Daylight.
Music.

Fallon and Broom are walking slowly up the middle of the street
towards us, looking all around them with a nudging delight.
Broom wears a new extravagant cravat, but still keeps to his ruffian's
coat.
Fallon has tied a gipsy-coloured kerchief round his neck.
We do not hear any of the street noises. This is a brief, silent
scene, to music.
People are walking past them, up and down the street. An elegant
old lady goes by. Broom side grins, points his finger after her.
A nursemaid with two children passes on their other side. And
Fallon wags his head in their direction. For their own enjoyment,
with winks and nudges, they point out in dumb show various of
the passers-by, especially the elderly and the very young.

DISSOLVE to

76

Murray sitting, alone, in the DISSECTING ROOM.

Night.

A drawing block is on his knees.

We see, over his shoulder, the drawing on the block.

It is a half-finished drawing of Jennie Bailey, lying as though asleep.
   Murray goes on drawing.   Now, on the paper, we see take shape
   one arm that hangs over the edge of the table, over the edge of
   her last bed.

Now Murray is drawing the clenched hand of the hanging arm.

And from the picture we *TRACK UP* towards the real hand.

And suddenly the hand unclenches itself: an after-death jerk of the
   nerves.

And two pennies fall out of the now open hand, and drop on to the
   floor.   We see them roll along the floor.

77

LARGE LODGING-ROOM.

Nelly and Kate are tidying the room, sweeping dirt into corners,
   covering up tousled beds with mud-coloured blankets, stopping
   to drink from a bottle on the broken table in the centre of the room.

We hear, from outside, the sound of a knock on the door.

Kate wipes her lips on her shawl and tucks the bottle inside her
   cabby-like layers of clothes.

    KATE. More lodgers!

She goes out of the room by the far door.

Nelly tipsily tidies herself, spits in her hand to help straighten a
   hanging lock of stiff hair.

And Kate comes back with a big, old, ragged beggar-man shuffling
   behind her, all dirt and hair, like a tame, tired, time- and whip-
   and weather-beaten bear.

    KATE. You can sleep in any bed you like dad, for twopence
   a night.   Clean and comfy.

NELLY. Are you alone?

The Old Man nods his head.

> KATE. All alone in the world? Nobody to care about you at all?

The Old Man shakes his head.

> KATE. Ach, isn't it a shame. . . . Nobody to care if you 're alive or dead. . . .

Kate looks at Nelly.

> NELLY. Let the old man have his bed for a penny, Kate.

And Kate takes the Old Man's luggage—which is wrapped up in a handkerchief—and they each hold an arm and lead him over to the bed near the small-room door: the bed where the other Old Man died.

78

DINING-ROOM OF ROCK'S HOUSE.

Day.

Elizabeth, in dust-cap and apron, is cleaning the silver.

Suddenly there is the long pealing ring of a door bell. And Elizabeth puts down her cleaning cloth, hurriedly takes off her cap and apron, and goes out of the room, leaving the door open.

We hear the opening of the street door, and then the voices of Elizabeth and Murray.

> MURRAY. I hope I am not disturbing you, Mrs. Rock.
> ELIZABETH. Come in, please, Mr. Murray. Do you want to see Thomas? He's lecturing. Oh, you'd know that, of course. My sister-in-law 's upstairs. . . .
> MURRAY. I want to see *you*, if I may.

And Murray follows Elizabeth into the room.

> ELIZABETH. You shall see me cleaning the silver, then. . . .

She puts on her cap and apron again, and begins to polish the candlesticks on the table.

ELIZABETH. I thought it might be a stranger at the door. . . . That's why I had to take my cap and apron off. Miss Annabella would never forgive me if I went to the door dressed like this. . . . But it's only you. I needn't have worried, need I? . . .

MURRAY. I'm afraid that after I tell you what I have to tell you, you will never want to see me again. . . .

ELIZABETH. [Smiling.] Oh no, no, nothing could be as bad as that. . . . What has Thomas been doing now? Writing terrible letters to the papers, or telling all the young men to put gunpowder under the City Hall?

MURRAY. No, ma'am.

ELIZABETH. *I* don't mind, you know. . . . It's only—some other people mind. Thomas can write or say anything he likes: I don't *understand* very much of it. . . . What have you got to tell me?

MURRAY. [Slowly, deliberately.] I believe that Thomas has instructed two men called Fallon and Broom to commit murder and to sell him the bodies.

There is a silence. Elizabeth stands still, half turned away from Murray. Then:

ELIZABETH. That is a—*horrible* lie. If Thomas hears it . . .

MURRAY. He *has* heard it.

Elizabeth begins again to polish the candlesticks. She still does not look at Murray.

MURRAY. Yesterday the body of a young woman called Jennie Bailey was delivered to the Academy by Fallon and Broom. Less than twelve hours before, I had seen her outside the theatre, alive and well. It is not possible that she could have died a natural death.

ELIZABETH. Can't people die a 'natural death' in twelve hours?

And under Elizabeth's calm voice there is a new hardness. There is a tenseness in all her smallest movements as she cleans and

74

polishes, not turning round. She is, quite suddenly, not a sweet and mild young woman but a protectress and an enemy.

MURRAY. She did not die a natural death.

ELIZABETH. Was this 'young woman' strangled, or stabbed, or shot, or poisoned, or beaten to death?

MURRAY. [In a slow, low voice, as though he had said the words over and over to himself.] There were no marks of violence upon the body. . . .

We see Elizabeth's relief expressed in the relaxing of the tenseness of the muscles of her shoulders. And now she turns round to face Murray.

ELIZABETH. And so you have no proof at all. . . . How could you? Why did you come to me with such a story? You should go to the police. . . .

MURRAY. I believe that she was smothered to death in such a way as to leave no signs. . . . I came to you first, because I want you to tell Thomas that he must go away. At once. Out of the country. I owe him a great deal. I would not care to see him hanged.

ELIZABETH. You are very kind. . . . Have you thought about yourself? Run out now and shout your lies in the streets, and they will lock you up because you are a mad-man. Or run to all the lawyers and justices, and they'll ask you for proof and you won't have any: and they'll lock you up because you bear false witness against your neighbour. Or go around in the dark, whispering all the foul things in your own mind to everybody that will listen, and you'll make such a panic and scare that Thomas's school will have to close and all the people who had anything to do with it will be stoned and spat upon and driven out. And you'll never, never, never again be allowed to work in any hospital or any school or anywhere. And nobody will ever speak to you again, or touch you, or be seen anywhere in the world with you. . . .

MURRAY. I have thought of that. I have thought of everything.

75

ELIZABETH. And if you call Thomas a murderer, everybody will call you murderer, too. They will call you murderer and butcher. . . .

MURRAY. All I know is that if Thomas did not *tell* these men to murder, he bought the bodies *knowing* that they were murdered.

ELIZABETH. I thought Thomas told me that it was one of *your* duties to buy the bodies. Will *that* help you very much when you accuse him? Will you go to the police now? Will you tell people what you 've told me? It will be quite easy for you to wreck your life, and his, and mine! I shan't try to stop you.

MURRAY. What shall I do?

ELIZABETH. Keep quiet. You knew the girl—Jennie Bailey?

MURRAY. Yes.

ELIZABETH. What was she?

MURRAY. She was a girl from the market. . . .

ELIZABETH. Was she pretty?

Murray nods, slowly.

ELIZABETH. I think I remember her if she was the girl outside the theatre. She was—*beautiful*. You liked her very much?

MURRAY. Yes.

ELIZABETH. I think you liked her so much that when she died you—lost your head. You didn't know what you were doing or what you were saying. Do you understand? You *imagined things*. Do you understand?

Annabella comes in.

ANNABELLA. Good afternoon, Mr. Murray. I didn't know any one had called. I see my sister-in-law is entertaining you. . . .

ELIZABETH. Mr. Murray called to see if Thomas was here. He had something to discuss with him. But now he says it doesn't matter. . . . Does it, Mr. Murray?

And Murray looks, without speaking, at the faces of the two women.

79

INTERIOR OF TAVERN B, FROM THE ANGLE OF THE DOOR.

Broom is standing in the middle of the room, looking around him.
There are few customers.

In one corner, alone, wrapped up as though against the cold, we
recognize Alice. She raises her head, sees Broom, clutches her
shawl more tightly round her, and turns her head away to the wall.

And we see Billy Bedlam sitting, also alone, staring at an empty mug
before him.

Broom flicks a coin in the air, catches it in the palm of his hand,
looks down into his palm. Then he crosses to Billy.

CLOSE SHOT of Billy and Broom.

> BROOM. Would you be having a little drink, Billy?

Billy smiles up, trustfully, delighted.

> BROOM. [Without turning from Billy, in a high, loud voice.]
> Two gins. [Then ingratiatingly.] It's you and me could
> drink the sea dry, Billy, and eat the fishes and cuddle the
> mermaids and dance a jig and play the penny whistle
> and . . .

The potman comes up with the drinks. Broom pays as he talks, and
the potman goes off.

They drink them off in a gulp.

> BILLY. I've seen a shark. . . .
> BROOM. [Loudly.] Two gins. [Softly.] You could wrestle
> the shark and toss him over your head like a pound of
> cat's-meat. . . . You're strong, Billy. . . .

The potman comes up with the drinks. Broom pays as he talks,
and the potman goes off.

They drink them off in a gulp.

> BILLY. I know a riddle. . . .
> BROOM. Tell Broom your riddle. . . . Two drinks!
> BILLY. In what month of the year do the ladies talk least?

77

BROOM. Oh, that's a good one. And what month *would* it be, Billy?

BILLY. The month of February, because there wiz least days in it.

And Broom raises his head and yelps with laughter; and slaps his thigh, and cracks his fingers.

Delighted, Billy splutters and crows.

BROOM. Tell Broom a riddle, Billy . . . another riddle. . . .

Broom beckons over his shoulder in the direction of the bar, then leans close to Billy again.

BILLY. I can tell you a riddle that nobody knows and nobody can guess it. . . .

BROOM. What is it, Billy?

BILLY. Though I black an' dirty am,
    An' black as black can be,
    There's many a lady that will come
    And by the hand tak' me.

Now you can't guess that. . . .

BROOM. Ah no, Billy, I can't guess that fickly one. Who learned you all those fickly guesses?

BILLY. It wiz my half step-mither. Oh, she's a cunning old body! Oh, she's cunning as a kitten when we're all sitting beside her round the fireside. She tells us a million million million funny stories, but I don't remember them all. . . .

    Though I am black an' dirty an' . . .

BROOM. It's a tea-kettle. . . .

BILLY. [Almost in tears.] Somebody told you.

BROOM. Well, tell us another, *Royal* Billy. . . .

And he beckons over his shoulder, towards the counter, for more drink, and leans again across the table to listen to Billy.

BROOM. And we'll drink . . . and we'll drink . . . and we'll . . .

And his voice softens and softens until it fades.

SMALL ROOM IN LODGING-HOUSE.

Candles in bottles on the table.

We see, in a corner, the pile of old rags and bones. It is far higher than when we last saw it.

Kate lies half on, half off the straw bed near the wall.

Nelly is looking out of the window. The window is open. From outside we hear the squealing of pigs.

The door is flung open.

Broom and Billy lurch in.

Nelly turns from the window.

We hear her whisper:

> NELLY. Not Billy Bedlam!
> BROOM. [To Nelly.] Shut the window. The pigs is too loud. It sounds like a killing. . . .

Nelly shuts the window.

> BROOM. And bring out a bottle for Billy. . . .

Billy staggers to a chair in a corner, sits on it, tilts it back on two legs and smiles at Nelly, who is staring at him as she brings out a bottle from a cupboard near the window.

> BILLY. He bought me snuff. . . .

Billy opens his box of snuff. Half of it spills over him. He scrabbles it off his clothes.

And Broom takes the bottle from Nelly and carries it over to Billy and gives it to him and watches him drink.

We see Billy's face as he drinks: drunkenly made beautiful.

But we see only the back of the watching Broom, and he does not turn round as he speaks:

> BROOM. Go round the shebeens and find Fallon. Tell him there's business.

Nelly goes to the door; she looks over her shoulder at Billy.

From her angle we see Billy and Broom's back.

BILLY. He gave me snuff. . . .

    He gave me snuff and whisky. . . .

    He promised me a shilling. . . .

BROOM. [Still not looking round.] And a sleep. . . .

And, looking at Broom's back and at Billy, we hear the door close.

81

INTERIOR OF TAVERN A.

CLOSE SHOT of Fallon sitting at a table, a mug before him.
His face is covered with sweat.
And terror looks out of his eyes.
He raises his hands before him, palms upward.   They are trembling.
His lips are moving, but no words come.
TRACK BACK to see Nelly sitting down next to him.

    NELLY. Broom says you're to come.

Fallon stares in front of him.

    NELLY. He says there's . . . work.

    FALLON. [Without turning to her.] My hands have worked
        enough.   There's devils in my hands.

    NELLY. It's . . . somebody we know Broom's got there. . . .

    FALLON. I've known them all, all of them.   They were my
        brothers . . . and my sisters . . . and my mother. . . .
        [In a horrified whisper.] . . . All dead . . . dead. . . .

    NELLY. Hurry up with you. . . . Broom's waiting. . . .

Fallon does not move.

    NELLY. You've drunk yourself daft again . . . like when you
        went on your knees in the street, praying and shouting. . . .

    FALLON. I wish I was workin' again, on the roads, on the
        canals, anywhere. . . .

    NELLY. D'you want us all to starve while you blather and
        weep your eyes out. . . .

    FALLON. Starving's better than these . . .

And he raises his hands again . . . and suddenly tautens them.

And Nelly pulls roughly, violently, at his sleeve, and drags him up, and pushes him out of the door into the darkness.

82

SMALL ROOM IN LODGING-HOUSE.

We see the room from the angle of the window.

Billy is still sprawling on the tilted chair in the corner.

Broom leans against the table, arms folded, watching Billy. He leans with his head a little to one side, enjoying the spectacle: a freak admiring a freak show.

Kate is still lying half on, half off the bed, her hand trailed in a puddle on the floor.

> BROOM. [Softly.] And when Mr. Fallon comes back, oh, we'll have fun and singing. . . . It's he's got a voice that'll send you to sleep like your mother's. . . . And oh, the joking and riddles!

PAN ROUND to the door as Broom speaks. Fallon is standing there. Behind him, almost in darkness, we see Nelly.

Fallon stands there at the door with his shoulders back and his head high. There is something almost of dignity about him: something that might suggest he is about to make a sacrifice.

And when he speaks, it is without the usual blarneying whine; a horror that has reached him has deepened the tone of his voice.

> FALLON. [Slowly.] Make Kate go.

Now, from Nelly's angle, behind Fallon, we see Broom move across to the bed in two cat-padded jumps and pinch Kate awake.

She looks round the room, thick with sleep. She sees Billy smiling at every one and no one; she sees the malicious face of Broom above her; she sees Fallon grim in the doorway. And, sober in a second, and frightened, she scrambles to the door.

Fallon does not move; she has to squeeze herself past him, keeping her body as far away from his as she can.

> FALLON. Close the door.

CUT to shot, from behind Billy, over his crippled shoulders, of Fallon at the door and Broom by the bed.

Fallon's eyes are staring straight at us.

    FALLON. [Slowly.] You mustn't be frightened, Billy.

Fallon takes a step forward.

    FALLON. [Slowly.] It 'll all be over soon. No more bein' hungry. . . .

Now Fallon, slow as a priest, is moving towards us and Billy.

CUT to shot, from door, of Fallon moving towards Billy, and of Billy's bewildered, but still smiling, face. . . .

    FALLON. [Slowly.] No more . . . cold. . . .

CUT to shot, from Billy's angle, of Fallon moving, as though in procession, down the room.

And behind him, on tiptoes, comes Broom. Now they are almost upon us.

And suddenly we hear the voice of Billy: screaming.

83

OUTSIDE THE DOOR OF THE SMALL ROOM.

Nelly and Kate are standing close to the door.

A little light, as though from one candle, falls on their faces.

Around them, darkness.

The women stand tensed, waiting, close together. And from beyond the door comes Billy's scream.

The scream mounts, breaks, and bursts out again. The crash of a falling chair.

And now it is not a scream that comes from beyond the door but a terrified howling; and with it the sound of a deeper voice: Fallon's voice—the voice of the damned inarticulately praying. And with it the smashing of wood, and glass breaking.

Then one scream destroys all other sounds.

The women put their hands over their ears, press their hands hard.

And the women are rocking slowly to and fro, as though at the side
   of a death-bed, as though at a wailing-wall.
Then the scream goes out.
Slowly the women grow still, and they move their hands down.
The door opens.
Light falls upon the white-faced women.
Fallon stands at the door with his back to the room, so that we
   cannot see his face or the room behind him.
Fallon raises his hand to beckon the women in.
He turns around, goes into the light.
The women go after him, so that the doorway is never unoccupied
   and so that we do not see into the room.
Then the door closes.

FADE OUT.

FADE IN

84

Birds flying over the City roofs.
Morning.
Music.
PAN DOWN from the roofs to the MARKET-PLACE.
As we *PAN*, we hear the voices of children rising.
And children are playing in the middle of the Market.
Then there is the clop-clop of hooves on cobbles.   And down the
   Market comes a horse and cart.
As the horse and cart approach us, we see that Fallon is driving.
There is a large barrel in the back of the cart.   Broom is thumping
   the barrel in time to the hoof-beats on the cobbles.
The children scatter as the cart drives down.
And then the horse stops.
Fallon raises a stick and beats the horse.
The horse will not move.
Broom stops his rhythmic thumping on the barrel and stands up.

He shouts at Fallon and the horse in his piercing voice, and the scampering children gather round the cart.

BROOM. Beat the hide off his back, skin the divil alive. . . .

Fallon beats the horse methodically, as though it were a carpet.

THE CHILDREN. Skin the divil alive.

BROOM. Oh, the mule of hell, the stinkin' gob of the knackers' yard, I'll tear off its tail. . . .

THE CHILDREN. Tear off its tail, tear off its tail. . . .

Fallon climbs off the cart and tries to drag the horse along by its bridle.

The horse will not move. And as Fallon drags and pulls, so Broom in the cart capers and cries, and so the children in delight caper and cry with Broom.

The people of the Market look on with little interest.

BROOM. I'll tear the bit out its mouth. . . . Give me a red⁄hot poker. . . .

THE CHILDREN. Red⁄hot poker, red⁄hot poker. . . .

FALLON. [Solemnly.] You'd think the old mare had risen in judgment against us. . . .

A Porter passes the horse and cart, pushing an empty barrow. He pays no heed to the caterwauling of Broom and the children.

Fallon sees the Porter.

FALLON. Hi, there!

The Porter stops.

BROOM. I'll kick it in the kyte. . . .

FALLON. Would you take a barrel with you for two shillings? It's only a little barrel. . . .

PORTER. Where to? It's a great big barrel. . . .

FALLON. My friend'll show you where.

Fallon beckons Broom, who has now stopped cursing the horse and is snapping like a dog at the children.

FALLON. Here's the shillings.

84

And Fallon, Broom, and the Porter lift the barrel down and put it
on the barrow. As they carry it the Porter says:

> PORTER. What you got in the barrel?
> BROOM. Potatoes.
> FALLON. Keep your talk in your mouth. You 've got your
> money. . . .

And Broom and the Porter go off with the barrow.

And suddenly the horse, as soon as the barrow has gone, goes off
himself down the Market, to the cries of the children, at a brisk trot.

Fallon shouts after it, but it trots on.

> THE CHILDREN. Skin the divil alive. . . . Tear off its tail,
> tear off its tail. . . Kick it in the kyte. . . .

Fallon, after one shout, makes no attempt to follow the horse but
walks back in the direction from which he had come; walks off
heavy-shouldered and heavy-footed, his head sunken.

The voices of the children fade.

85

RAG-AND-BONE ALLEY.

TRACK UP to where a middle-aged man and woman are standing
outside the door of the Lodging-house. The woman carries a
baby in a shawl. The man holds a little child by the hand.
They are dressed like beggars. The man is carrying a bundle in
a stick over his shoulder. He knocks at the door.

> WOMAN. It 's a poor, dirty place.
> MAN. It 's got a roof. . . .
> WOMAN. I think I 'd rather be on the roads, sleeping in the
> hedge in the cold. . . .

The door opens.

Kate stands in the doorway.

She wears a new shawl.

> KATE. You 'll be wanting a bed? They 're twopence.
> MAN. Bed.

The man unwraps a piece of cloth from his pocket, and brings out a coin.

> KATE. There's nobody sleeping at all here now. . . . You can take your fancy where you sleep. . . .

The man and the woman follow her into the house and into:

The Lodging-Room.

Even in daylight it is half dark. . . .

Kate walks down the room, and the man and the woman follow her.

> KATE. You're strangers here. . . .
> MAN. Strangers everywhere. . . .
> KATE. You're from the roads?

The man nods.

> WOMAN. I think we won't be troubling you for a bed. . . . It's *dark* here. . . .
> KATE. It's darker on the roads. With no one you know in the world, and no one to take care of you. . . . I'll make the beds a penny each. What names d' you go by?
> MAN. Mr. and Mrs. Webb.
> WOMAN. We're respectable people. . . .
> KATE. We're all respectable here. Just my husband and me. He's in the way of a merchant. . . .

The man flings his bundle on a bed. And Kate looks at Mr. and Mrs. Webb.

86

CITY STREET.

The Porter is pushing his barrow along, Broom at his side.

> PORTER. You're sure you said it was potatoes in your—*little* barrel?

Broom winks.

PORTER. They're very heavy potatoes. Where do we go with them?

BROOM. Up the City square. Doctor Rock's Academy.

PORTER. [With a sideways glance at Broom.] He must be very fond of vegetables. . . .

87

HALLWAY OF ROCK'S ACADEMY.

Night.

The Hallway is deserted.

The door to the small Cloak-room under the stairs stands open.

Murray comes out of the Cloak-room.

He looks around him, like a man slowly coming out of a nightmare and trying to grow accustomed again to the familiar things of the daytime world.

MURRAY. Tom! Tom! Where are you, Tom?

But it is only a whisper.

And now he walks up the Hallway past the glass cases slowly.

He opens the door, and walks out through the colonnade into the moonlit garden of City Square. And as he moves through the garden so we hear the voice of his mind, and the remembered voices of others.

MURRAY'S VOICE. Who brought the subject in, Tom? There's no need to ask.

TOM'S VOICE. Fallon and Broom, sir; Fallon and Broom. . . .

MURRAY'S VOICE. What can I do?

ELIZABETH'S VOICE. Keep quiet. . . .

MURRAY'S VOICE. Keep quiet about Jennie or they'll lock you up. . . .

ELIZABETH'S VOICE. Keep quiet. . . .

MURRAY'S VOICE. Keep quiet about Billy Bedlam in the little room, or they'll call you a murderer and a butcher. . . .

ELIZABETH'S VOICE. . . . stabbed or strangled, or beaten to death, or . . .

MURRAY'S VOICE. There are no marks of violence upon the body.

ELIZABETH'S VOICE. . . . You bear false witness. . . .

MURRAY'S VOICE. I swear that Jennie and Billy are murdered. . . .

ELIZABETH'S VOICE. It is quite easy for you to wreck your life. . . .

And he turns and walks back through the garden towards the Academy. Now his step is quicker and more purposeful.

88

ELIZABETH'S ROOM.

Rock, his coat off, but still immaculately dressed, is seated in a deep chair with his head against the back of it.

Elizabeth is curling what remains of his hair with curling-tongs.

Rock has an air of indolent luxury.

ROCK. [Complacently.] The sensual apotheosis of the intellectual animal. . . .

ELIZABETH. If you say so, my dear.

ROCK. The mind is relaxed, the body is pleasured and pampered, rancour has taken a holiday, and I am full of bliss, like a cat on the tiles of heaven. . . .

ELIZABETH. It must be very nice to talk. . . .

ROCK. It is comparable only to the pleasure of not having to think *as* you talk. . . . [Sighing.] I am a fool to-day.

ELIZABETH. Yes. Thomas . . .

ROCK. [With a change of voice.] But not so much of a fool as some I know. That rumour-breeder of a Murray! Falls in love with a pretty face and then won't cut it up once the little trollop's dead. Says she's murdered. Says, in effect, I murdered her myself.

ELIZABETH. [Mildly.] Oh, Thomas.

ROCK. When *I* take up assassination, I shall start with the surgeons in this city and work *up* to the gutter. . . . And

88

now, to-day, along he comes with some fantastic rigmarole about a crippled idiot. Billy Bedlam. Says *he*'s murdered, too. Poor Billy's bed was the cobbles, rain or snow, and he ate like a rat from the garbage heaps, and swallowed all the rot-gut he could buy or beg. He was a consumptive and an epileptic. A wonder he hadn't been found dead years ago. . . .

ELIZABETH. What did you tell Mr. Murray?

ROCK. I said: 'Mr. Murray, go down and cut up the body and put it in the brine baths. Be careful you don't fall in yourself—you're wearing a good suit!'

ELIZABETH. [Casually.] And what did he do?

ROCK. What did he do? Why, what I told him to do, of course. No vicious-minded little prig with emotional adenoids is going to intimidate *me* with his whine and wail of 'Murder! Murder!' He suffers from hallucinations. My hands, to him, are red as Macbeth's. . . .

Rock raises his very white hands in an elegant gesture, and smoothes the palm of one hand along the back of the other. . . .

89

Music.

Pitch darkness.

Through the darkness, the laughter of Broom.

Then sudden light, and Fallon's hands, palms downwards, fingers stretched and tautened, murdering down the screen.

As the hands move we hear Fallon's voice, blurred in a distorting mirror of sound.

> FALLON'S VOICE. There's devils in my hands. Let me go, my hands!

Then, close, from above, the upward-staring faces of old women and children, their eyes wide, their mouths open.

> FALLON'S VOICE. Don't be frightened. . . . There's nothing to lose. . . .

Then Fallon's hands, palms upwards, fingers damp and limp, trembling up the screen.

FALLON'S VOICE. It's all lost. . . .

Then CLOSE-UP of Fallon's face, drunk, arrogant, grinning.
And we hear a voice questioning the face.

VOICE. And where d' you get all the money so quick? You're rich, you're *rich*, you're . . .

FALLON'S VOICE. Ach, I done a little smuggling; a little bit o' drink on the sly. . . .

The questioning Voice continues through a CLOSE-UP of Nelly in a new feathered bonnet. Nelly drunk, secretive. . . .

VOICE. And where d' you get all the money so quick? You're *rich*, you're . . .

NELLY'S VOICE. Oh, I've been left a property in the country.

CLOSE-UP of Kate in a new bonnet.

VOICE. And where d' you get all the money . . . [The Voice fades.]

KATE'S VOICE. Oh, Fallon's the favourite of a great lady. . . . *Twenty* pounds a visit she gives him. . . .

Then CLOSE-UP of children's faces.

VOICE. Where's Billy? Billy Bedlam?

And the voices of the children answer as we see a CLOSE-UP of Alice.

VOICES OF CHILDREN. Gone, gone . . .
VOICE. Where's Jennie? Jennie Bailey?

And Alice's voice answers as we see a CLOSE SHOT of a sack put down and hands undoing the sack.

ALICE'S VOICE. Gone, gone . . .

And out of the undone sack comes a human arm, and we hear the voice of the Porter.

PORTER'S VOICE. Doctor Rock is very fond of vegetables. . . .

CLOSE SHOT of an Old Man, drooling drunk, his head capsized on one shoulder.

> BROOM'S VOICE. Drink with Broom. . . . Drink. . . .

A hand with a bottle in it stretches across the screen towards him.
CUT to *CLOSE-UP* of the face of an Old Woman looking up at the bottle held across the screen.

> BROOM'S VOICE. Drink . . . drink. . . .

And, loudly, there is the noise of the pigs squealing.

DISSOLVE the picture to

90

INTERIOR OF GROCER'S SHOP.

From the end of the shop, opposite the door, we can see a section of the Market-place in daylight.

The Grocer, behind the counter, is a truculent man in a dirty apron, who seems to have given up hope a long time ago: a man always at the end of his patience.

And before the counter an Old Woman is standing, wrapped in pieces of the discarded clothing of the other poor.

> GROCER. For the last time, I don't know a Flynn. . . .
>
> OLD WOMAN. Timothy Boylan Flynn. . . .
>
> GROCER. I don't know a Flynn, I've never known a Flynn, I never want to . . .
>
> OLD WOMAN. From County Donegal. . . . He came over two years ago and a half. . . . He's a tall, dark boy. . . . The lobes of his ears is pointed. . . .

Fallon comes in at the shop door. He stands, framed against the Market, listening.

> GROCER. 'What's the time of the day?' 'Can you give me a wooden box?' 'My sister's fallen under a hay cart—can you lend me a penn'orth of brandy.' 'Have you seen a Flynn?' Will nobody ever *buy* anything? . . .
>
> OLD WOMAN. Could you spare me a bite o' bread, then?

91

The Grocer controls himself as Fallon, with a winning smile, comes to the counter.

FALLON. [To the Old Woman.] Did I hear you say 'Flynn'? That was my mother's name.

OLD WOMAN. From Ardara, Donegal?

FALLON. [Amazed.] Ardara, Donegal! My mother's town! And would *your* name be—Flynn, too?

GROCER. *Her* name's Flynn, she's *looking* for a Flynn, and now your *mother's* name is Flynn. . . .

Fallon, still looking at the Old Woman, hands an earthenware jug over the counter to the Grocer.

FALLON. Fill it up with dew.

The Grocer disappears behind the counter.

FALLON. [Affectionately to the Old Woman.] Then you're my little cousin. . . .

He kisses her forehead. . . .

FALLON. Cousin Flynn. . . .

Faith, what a day of all days! I'm walking along gay as a thrush, I'm fragrant with the sweet smell of money, to-night's Hallowe'en when the witches fly and the whisky pours like rain, and who should I meet on top of it all but a Flynn from Ardara!

The Grocer returns to his place behind the counter; he hands over the earthenware jug to Fallon. Fallon, tossing coins carelessly on the counter, pays for it; but he does not take his eyes off Mrs. Flynn. . . .

MRS. FLYNN. It's my son for I'm looking all over, sir. . . .

FALLON. [Emphatically.] . . . Cousin. . . .

MRS. FLYNN. [Hesitatingly.] . . . Cousin. . . .

FALLON. And we'll find your son for you if we have to pull the town down and scramble among the cobbles. . . .

You come with me, cousin . . . you're welcome as sunlight. . . . I'll buy you a present for Hallowe'en, and I'll take you back to my fine house and we'll kick up a din like all Donegal drunk. . . .

Fallon, with the jug and Mrs. Flynn, moves towards the door of the
  shop, towards the darkening Market.

As they go out we see a *CLOSE SHOT* of the Grocer.

> GROCER. [With an awful resignation.] Hallowe'en! . . .

91

RAG-AND-BONE ALLEY.

Late evening.

Music.

The Close is desolate.

We hear the dark noise of the wind blowing.

The noise grows, but the Close is emptily still.

The wind rises, to the rise of music.

And out of the gutters float the wind-driven shapes of witches and
  demons:

Waste paper flying out of the gutter, eddying into the air, fluttering,
  as though winged, past the shadowy houses:

Paper and rubbish gusted suddenly from the cobbles to flap and
  float about the street, to beat against the windows and scrabble
  there, to rise on the screaming breath of a wind and drift before the
  Lodging-house:

Straw blown in a squall, straw shapes and garbage shapes puffed
  through the growing, blowing dark:

Hay wisps and knotted straw, dust clouds and cloth shreds, small
  crumpled nameless shapes, light as paper and string, scudding
  through the narrowness:

All the inanimate furies of the Close alive suddenly, crying like the
  wind through telegraph wires, grotesque dancers from the dirt. . . .

92

Now we are standing at the end of the LARGE LODGING-ROOM.

We are looking down the mostly dark long room and through the
  open door into the small room.

We hear laughter, and snatches of singing, and a jig tune played on a penny whistle.

Broom and Kate, arm in arm, come dancing out of the small room, turn in the narrow aisle between the beds, and dance, singing, back. We *TRACK UP* slowly to the open door.

As we track we see that one of the beds is occupied: by a baby and a young child. They are the children of Mr. and Mrs. Webb. They are asleep. The child's arm is held protectingly around the baby.

Now we are near the open door.

We see, in the small room, Fallon leaning against the table, playing a whistle. There are cups and mugs on the table, bottles, and the earthenware jug.

Behind Fallon are a man and a woman: a squat and hairy man not unlike Fallon, and a slatternly young woman with wayward hair and smile.

And Broom and Mrs. Flynn, arm in arm, come dancing out of the small room, towards us.

We see them close as they turn in the narrow aisle between the beds.

Mrs. Flynn is gay as an old cat.

Broom is smiling and possessive.

They dance, singing, back into the small room.

We *TRACK* right up to the open door.

In the small room we see that there are nine people: Fallon, penny-whistling at the table; the two strangers behind him singing the words of a jig; Kate and Nelly on the straw bed, beating jig-time on the littered floor; Broom and Mrs. Flynn dancing between the table and the bed, dancing around the table; and Mr. and Mrs. Webb. Mr. Webb, with a look of bemused contentment, is soaking pieces of bread in the earthenware jug and eating them; Mrs. Webb, disapproving, sits on the edge of the one sound chair in the room.

Mrs. Webb complains, through the singing, the dancing, the floor-beating, and the whistling.

MRS. WEBB. Oh, the noise, it 'll wake all the neighbours. . . .

THE MAN. They wouldn't wake to-night if you set their clothes on fire. . . . All the city's drunk. . . .

MRS. WEBB. [To Mr. Webb.] And stop eatin' bread and gin; it's bad for the stomach.

BROOM. It's Hallowe'en. . . .

THE MAN. It isn't us who's only making the din, you listen now. . . . Shh!

The Man raises his hand. For a moment the room is quiet. The dancers pause. From outside we hear the noise of drunken singing, and voices bawling and brawling.

Then Fallon begins to play again, and Broom and Mrs. Flynn dance again, and the Man and the Woman sing, and Kate and Nelly, speechless on the bed, go on thumping.

MR. WEBB. Bread and gin's good for the stomach.

MRS. WEBB. You'll be waking the children, that's what'll happen next, with your caterwauling and your bang-bangs and your . . .

Fallon stops playing.

FALLON. And can't a man have a party now in honour of his cousin?

MR. WEBB. And rum and spuds is good.

FALLON. [To Mrs. Webb.] You're an auld spoil-sport, Mrs. Webb, you'd stop the dead dancin' on Judgment Day. . . .

The baby, from the next room, begins to scream.
Mrs. Webb jumps up and goes out.
But the screaming continues.

FALLON. Now that's a baby that likes good music. . . .

And he raises his penny whistle and plays again.
Mrs. Webb puts her head round the door.

MRS. WEBB. For the Lord's sake now, is this a lodging house or a wake?

Fallon nods to Nelly.
And Nelly totters to her feet and goes out of the room.

95

93

In the LARGE LODGING-ROOM we see Nelly and Mrs. Webb at the
bed of the screaming baby.

Through the open door we see the singers and dancers.

> NELLY. Oh, the poor creature. It screams like it swallowed
> a pin. . . . And Fallon 'll be playing his whistle all
> night . . .

Through the open door we see Fallon whistling and dancing a
lonely jig.

> NELLY. . . . and there 'll not be a breath of peace. . . .
> [Wheedling.] Now why don't you take the children away
> for the night. . . . Fallon's brother there will give you a
> bed and a plate of food. . . . And Fallon and us 'll stay
> singing with old Mrs. Flynn till we a' fall down. . . .

The baby screams louder than ever.

> MRS. WEBB. [Calling through the door.] Come on with ye,
> Mr. Webb.

Mrs. Webb begins to lift the children out of bed and wrap clothes
around them.

94

Through darkness we see a shivering candle move, and moving
figures. The baby is still screaming.

> MR. WEBB. I don't want to go out in the cold. . . .
> MRS. WEBB. You and your bread and gin! . . .
> THE MAN. Only a couple of steps from here, Mrs. Webb. . . .
> MR. WEBB. It's Hallowe'en! . . .
> NELLY. I think you 're very wise to go, my dear. There's no
> knowing what pranks Mr. Fallon 'll be up to to-night. . . .

A door is opened.

We see Rag-and-Bone Alley in the moonlight.

And the Man and the Woman, and Mr. and Mrs. Webb and the
baby and the child, go out into the moonlight.

And Nelly closes the door.

Pitch darkness. From the darkness a sudden swell of sound: the squealing and squeaking of the tin whistle, and the singing of Broom.

Then momentary quiet.

Then Broom's singing again, and, suddenly through it, a long, high, distant cry dwindling into silence again.

95

Snow falling in hard, bright morning light.

Nothing on the screen but the falling snow. We hear a cock crow.

We *CUT* to a cock, on a wall, crowing in the middle of the snow, defiantly crying the morning up to the thick, falling flakes.

And now, as the snow drifts and drives past our eyes, we are looking, from the outside, through the Lodging-house window into the small room.

Isolated, behind the shifting wall of snow, sit Fallon and Broom, Nelly and Kate, at the table in the middle of the room. Only Fallon is not eating.

We move through the snow and through the window into the room and towards the table.

We see the details of the room very clearly now in the merciless morning snow-light: no shadows, no twisted shapes in half-darkness, but only the bed with its straw guts straggling out, and the fouled straw-heap on the floor at the foot of the bed, and the thrown-away bottles and the flung scraps of clothes, and the broken glass and the drying pools of drink, and the last and the snippets of leather, and the tin whistle cast near the straw, and the piled boots in the corner, and the iron pot near the smoking fire.

Then Fallon rises from the table and crosses to the window.

From behind him, looking over his tensed shoulders, we see the falling snow.

FALLON. The snow won't ever stop. It's like the last day.

And his voice, and his measured movements, and the concentrated stillness of the others, suggest the anticlimax after death.

And now, from the end of the room opposite the door, we see the door open and Mr. and Mrs. Webb come in. Their clothes are white with snow.

Broom leaps to his feet. Fallon turns, with a measured, deliberate movement from the window.

Nelly and Kate sit still at the table, looking up at Mrs. Webb.

>BROOM. [With a frightening smile.] You frightened us.

And he goes out of the room, followed by Kate.

>NELLY. You 're early.

>MRS. WEBB. I been up and about since dawn; the baby
>wouldn't fall to sleep at all—it screamed like things were
>after it. . . .

Fallon stands still at the window, looking at Mrs. Webb.

>NELLY. What have you come for so early?

>MRS. WEBB. I come to look for the little boy's stockings.
>I left them here last night drying by the fire; and I come
>for our bits and pieces. . . . It 's time we 're moving. . . .

Mrs. Webb is looking round the room.

She pulls out a clay pipe from her wrappings and lights it at the fire.

With the blackened pipe burning like a little hayrick in her mouth, she bends down and searches among the scraps of clothes on the floor near the straw.

>FALLON. Get away from that straw with your old pipe. . . .
>You 'll have the room blazing. . . .

Fallon speaks so harshly that Mrs. Webb takes an involuntary step backward and sits on the end of the bed.

>MR. WEBB. Where 's Mrs. Flynn? [Appreciatively.] She
>was a very gay old woman, dancin' like a nanny-goat. . . .

>NELLY. She was ow'r gay with Fallon. I tumbled her out
>of the house in the middle o' the night. . . .

>MR. WEBB. [With a side look at his wife.] I like a gay old
>woman. . . .

>FALLON. Get out o' my room. . . . Take your reeky scraps
>of rubbish and your yelpin' children and get out. . . .

Fallon does not move from the window, but his stillness is more menacing than movement.

And Mr. and Mrs. Webb go out.   As they go Mrs. Webb whines:

> MRS. WEBB. I want my little boy's stockings. . . .

Fallon is alone with Nelly.

> FALLON. The snow's falling heavier.
> The world's cold.

He shivers, pulls his coat closer about him.

> FALLON. It's cold in hell to-day.
> The fires are out.

Nelly looks at him in uncomprehending silence.

> FALLON. Nothing can burn me any more.
> I'm a cold man, Nelly.
> I'm numb all over, like an old dead finger-nail.
> No more dancing.
> No more drinking and singing.

He shivers again, standing against the window and the snow.

> FALLON. I got work to do.

And he goes out, followed by the strangely silent Nelly.

The door closes.

The room is empty.

Then the door opens, very slowly, and Mrs. Webb puts her head round and looks at the emptiness.

She comes in, whispering over her shoulder.

> MRS. WEBB. They've gone.

And Mr. Webb comes in, nervously glancing behind him and on every side.

> MR. WEBB. Find the stockings and let's be out of the house.

Mrs. Webb is down on her knees now by the pile of old clothes; she rummages through them.

> MRS. WEBB. Who wanted to come to this house? I said
> it was bad.   I could smell the badness as I come in.   It's
> nothing but drinking and howling all night. . . .

Suddenly she stops in her scrabbling search through the clothes
and lifts up a crumpled dress.

> MRS. WEBB. It's the old woman's dress.
>
> MR. WEBB. How'd she be walking in the streets in the snow
> without her dress?
>
> MRS. WEBB. It's the old woman's dress.   I mind the colour.

She starts to search among the clothes again, her hands nearing the
straw.

> MR. WEBB. A body doesna walk in the streets with-
> out her . . .

Mrs. Webb lifts up a ragged shawl.

> MRS. WEBB. And here's her little patchy shawl. . . .

Now she is worrying the straw, like a dog on a scent.

> MRS. WEBB. And here's her . . .

And Mrs. Webb screams.

A human arm lies naked in the parted straw.

Mrs. Webb springs up and stands, with her back to us, looking
down at the straw and the arm.

The scream stops.

Mr. Webb bends down; facing us, he flings the rest of the straw aside.
We do not see what he reveals, for Mrs. Webb stands between us and it.

> MR. WEBB. The gay old woman!   Her face is a' slimy.

Music.

Mrs. Webb rushes out of the room.

And, as Mr. Webb follows her, we see, for a flash, the dead white
face among the straw.

96

In the LARGE LODGING-ROOM Mr. and Mrs. Webb are frenziedly
packing their bits and pieces into a sheet.

The music rises.

They rush, he with the sheet sacked over his shoulder, to the far door.

And suddenly Nelly is standing there, in the doorway.
The music stops.

>NELLY. Where are you going? What have you seen?
>
>MRS. WEBB. Let me out, she's dead. . . .
>
>NELLY. She died in her sleep. . . .
>
>MR. WEBB. Her mouth's blood. . . .
>
>MRS. WEBB. For the love o' Mary . . .
>
>NELLY. *She died in her sleep.* . . .
>
>MRS. WEBB. . . . Let me out. . . .

Nelly tears inside her apron, pulls out a purse, opens it. She pushes
a handful of coins towards Mrs. Webb.

>NELLY. Nobody knows her, nobody'll claim her, you
>mustn't tell a word . . .
>
>MR. WEBB. Stand away . . .
>
>NELLY. . . . she died like a baby. . . .
>
>MRS. WEBB. You killed her in there last night. . . .
>
>NELLY. You musn't tell a word, mercy, quiet, quiet. . . .
>Fallon'll give you ten pounds, ten pounds a week . . .

Mr. Webb thrusts Nelly aside.
Mrs. Webb runs through the door, Mr. Webb after her.
Nelly, at the door, cries out after them . . .

>NELLY. Ten pounds . . .

97

RAG-AND-BONE ALLEY.

Music.
Snow falling heavily.
Mr. and Mrs. Webb rush out of the Lodging-house.
The Webbs' boy, with the baby in his arms, stands, waiting, like
a little snow man near the door.
Mrs. Webb snatches the baby from his arms, hugs it to her shawls,
and hurries on up the Alley.
Mr. Webb takes the boy's hand and follows.
They keep to the right of the Alley.

And down the left of the Alley, coming towards the Lodging-house, we see Fallon and Broom and a Porter.

But, with the fierce snow driving upon them, upon their faces and their eyes, they do not see the wrapped-up figures of the hurrying Webbs.

And the Webbs do not see them.

98

SMALL ROOM IN LODGING-HOUSE.

In the middle of the room is a tea-chest.

Fallon, Broom, and the Porter stand, snowy-coated, around the chest.

The Porter is the one we saw taking the barrel in his barrow.

He is pressing down the lid with all his weight.

And Fallon helps him.

Broom points a finger at the top of the lid.

A bunch of grey hair hangs out.

Fallon crosses to the last and the leather pieces and brings back a pair of cobbler's scissors.

The Porter cuts off the hair with the scissors.

99

INTERIOR OF POLICE STATION.

Mr. and Mrs. Webb are talking to a Policeman.

> MR. WEBB. And there was blood all over her face. . . .
> POLICEMAN. Aye.
> MRS. WEBB. And her poor lips were blue and her eyes were staring out as though somebody'd pressed 'em with his thumbs. . . .

The Policeman nods.

> MR. WEBB. She said she came from Donegal. . . .
> POLICEMAN. The 'dead woman' told ye she'd come from Donegal?

100

CITY STREET.

We see Fallon and Broom walking, in the slanting snowstorm, by the side of the Porter and his barrow with the tea-chest on it.

101

INTERIOR OF POLICE STATION.

Mr. and Mrs. Webb are still pleading to the Policeman.

> MR. WEBB. No, no, sir, she said she'd come from Donegal when we was all drinkin' together last night. . . .
> POLICEMAN. Drinkin'!
> MRS. WEBB. Mrs. Flynn her name was, I've told you twenty times. . . .

Mr. Webb, with hesitant, frightened fingers touches his own mouth.

> MR. WEBB. And now there's blood all over here. . . .
> POLICEMAN. [Placatingly.] You sit down now. I'll come with you by and by. . . .

He turns away from them and moves towards the back of the room.

> MRS. WEBB. [Dully, as though repeating a lesson.] Mrs. Flynn her name was. . . . They killed her. . . . Fallon and Broom. . . .

102

The always shadowy HALL in ROCK'S ACADEMY, with its white secret witnesses staring from the glass cases.

Rock is mounting the stairs.

We follow him as he climbs, and hear the voice of his mind.

> ROCK'S VOICE. Gentlemen. . . . Gentlemen, let us to-day dissect the human conscience. Lay it on the slab. Open it up.

You see? The liver of the conscience is knobbled by emotional excesses.

The veins of the conscience are full of bad blood.

The heart of the conscience palpitates like a snared rabbit's. . . .

Now he is walking along the Corridor, opening a door, to the small Reference Library.

103

REFERENCE LIBRARY IN ROCK'S ACADEMY.

ROCK'S VOICE. In short, gentlemen, the conscience is a *very* unhealthy subject. . . .

And, at the end of these words, he is sitting in a chair behind a desk, facing us.

The room is empty.

And Rock, at the desk, addresses the empty room as though there were a gathering of students in it, turning from one invisible listener to another.

ROCK. There is right and wrong, gentlemen, just as there is right and left. Mine is the *right* direction. The fact that the majority would consider it the *wrong* direction, only substantiates my opinion that I am right. . . .

There is a knock on the door.

ROCK. Stay out.

Tom comes in.

ROCK. I see, sir, that to keep you out I should have said, 'Come in.'

TOM. Fallon and Broom, sir.

ROCK. Indeed? Must I laugh, weep, tear my hair, swoon for ecstasy!

TOM. They 've brought a body, sir.

ROCK. I did not expect that they would bring a soul.

TOM. [Suggestively.] They bring so many subjects, sir . . .
    sixteen or more up till to-day . . . and always fresh. . . .
ROCK. They are corpse-diviners. Or, as some have green
    fingers for gardening, so they have black fingers for death.
    Do you expect the dead to walk here, Tom? They need
    assistance. Fallon and Broom provide that assistance.
        Have Mr. Murray pay them.
TOM. Yes, sir.

Tom, with a side glance at Rock, goes out.
And Rock, alone, again speaks in a soft voice to his unseen audience.

    ROCK. You see, gentlemen?

104

SMALL ROOM IN LODGING-HOUSE.

We look at the room from above.
In the centre of the room stands the Policeman. Behind him,
    standing close together for protection, are Mr. and Mrs. Webb.
Fallon leans against the table, facing the Policeman.
And behind him are Kate, Nelly, and Broom.
They are frozen.
As, from above, we move down closer to them, they unfreeze.

    FALLON. [Smiling.] And where did the old fools tell ye
        they saw the body, sir?

Mrs. Webb points to the straw.
The Policeman kicks the straw aside. Broom laughs.

    FALLON. Maybe the mice, they dragged it down their little
        hole. . . .

The Policeman bends down, to stare at the floor-boards.

    POLICEMAN. Blood on the boards.

A moment's silence.

    FALLON. And has there ever been, for the love o' God, a
        Hallowe'en party with no blood spilt? We was all con-
        vivial; there was fightin' in every room of the house.

NELLY. And the old woman Flynn, she was so fashous I told her go with the toe of my boot. . . .

KATE. [Pointing to the Webbs.] And it's they were picking the pockets of the poor innocent persons that couldn't get up from the floor. . . .

NELLY. It's all lies, lies they said. . . .

The Policeman picks up the dress that Mrs. Webb had found.

KATE. Don't you trust them, they're beggars, sir. . . .

BROOM. They eat dead cats. . . .

MRS. WEBB. That's Mrs. Flynn's dress. . . . I mind the colour. . . .

BROOM. Fur and all. . . .

NELLY. That's not hers, it's mine. . . .

POLICEMAN. Blood on the front.

NELLY. Fallon hit me with a glass in the face and the cut ran. . . .

MR. WEBB. The old woman's face was a' slimy. . . .

And as Mr. Webb speaks, so we hear the ringing of church bells. . . .

DISSOLVE.

105

Policeman and Mr. and Mrs. Webb with their two children walking up snow-thick STREET. Snow is no longer falling.

The sound of Sunday church bells rises.

And, black for Sunday, people hurry by over the white snow.

106

CITY SQUARE.

Outside Hocking's Academy Mr. and Mrs. Webb stand shivering and waiting, the baby huddled in Mrs. Webb's shawls, the little boy with his hands dug deep in Mr. Webb's coat pocket.

The door of Hocking's Academy opens.

The Policeman comes out.

A Porter stands at the door.

POLICEMAN. If there's a new subject comes in to-day, let me know.

He walks towards Rock's Academy, beckoning the Webbs to follow him.

He knocks on the door of Rock's Academy.

The grille opens.

From the Policeman's angle we see Tom's face through the bars.

POLICEMAN'S VOICE. Have you had a new subject to-day?

TOM. Aye.

POLICEMAN'S VOICE. Open the door.

The door opens.

The Policeman walks in.

107

SMALL DARK ROOM off the HALL in ROCK'S ACADEMY.

We see the figures of Tom and the Policeman, and the shape of the tea-chest.

POLICEMAN. Open the chest.

Tom opens the tea-chest.

The Policeman looks down into it.

POLICEMAN. When was it brought?

TOM. An hour ago.

POLICEMAN. Who brought it?

CUT to CLOSE-UP of Mrs. Flynn's face. With a sudden after-death jerk of the muscles, her mouth drops open, as though she were speaking.

And Tom speaks as the mouth opens.

TOM'S VOICE. Fallon and Broom.

CUT BACK to the small dark room, the Policeman, and Tom.

POLICEMAN. Fetch in the old couple. They're waiting outside.

Tom goes out.

The Policeman looks round the dark room. We follow his eyes:

we see, in a corner, what might be a body covered with a sheet: in another corner, what might be a cupboard or an upright coffin.

POLICEMAN. [In a whisper.] Cold!

Mr. and Mrs. Webb come into the room.
The Policeman nods towards the open tea-chest.
Timidly they move towards it and look down.

MR. WEBB. The old woman.

Mrs. Webb nods and crosses herself.

POLICEMAN. What was her name?

CUT again to CLOSE-UP of Mrs. Flynn's face.

MRS. WEBB'S VOICE. Mrs. Flynn. . . .

108

REFERENCE LIBRARY IN ROCK'S ACADEMY.

Rock, a sheet of paper in his hand, is walking up and down, in a characteristic lecture manner, behind his desk.
Some distance away, the other side of the desk, sits Murray.

ROCK. [Gesturing with the paper in his hand.] If this does not upset some apple-carts, I shall believe that the apples have been glued on like the coco-nuts in coco-nut shies; if this does not help to change the idiotic laws that apply to our profession, I shall run amok; I shall send Doctor Hocking a Christmas Greeting and sign it 'Yours in Homage'; I shall place my spiritual welfare in the hands of the Reverend Doctor Lever and have my seat *reserved* in hell.

MURRAY. I tell you, this isn't the time to attack.

ROCK. The national anthem of the rabbit world.

MURRAY. If you publish that letter now, attacking the system by which the medical schools get their bodies, you'll be raising a question you might have some difficulty in answering *yourself*.

ROCK. Am I still a Doctor Bluebeard to you, then, you terrified old lady? Do I spend my nights a-murdering?

MURRAY. I do not know, sir, what you do with your nights. I do not imagine that you can *sleep*. But I do know that *Fallon* and *Broom* are murderers. It is only my respect for you, and my great obligations, and my *cowardice*, that have stopped me from running out of this murder school and telling the whole city what I know and what I guess. . . . Even so, there are rumours. *I* have not spread them. But Jennie's death, and Billy's, have not passed *quite* unnoticed. Rumours are contagious.

ROCK. So are scabies. To destroy them you do not wear the armour of defence, you wield the weapon of sulphur ointment. And, by God, there's sulphur in this letter. . . .

Tom comes in.

TOM. The police have been here.

ROCK. What is yours, sir? A rum and bitters?

TOM. [Bewildered.] Sir?

ROCK. Since you do not knock before you come in, I must assume that this is a public-house. . . .

TOM. I beg your pardon, sir, but the police came about the new subject. Fallon and Broom, sir.

ROCK. Am I never to hear the end of those men's names?

MURRAY. [Softly.] Never, perhaps. . . .

TOM. And they're taking the subject away. . . .

ROCK. Why didn't you call the police? . . .

TOM. [More bewildered.] Sir, I . . .

ROCK. Go away and lock up the silver. If there isn't any silver, lock up Mr. Mattheson: he has a gold tooth.

And Tom goes out.

MURRAY. Must you antagonize every one?

ROCK. Yes.

MURRAY. You heard? The police.

ROCK. Outside the gates of hell are not the words 'Abandon Hope All Ye Who Enter Here,' but 'I Told You So.'

MURRAY. And if the police ask me questions, as they are
bound to do, what shall I say?

ROCK. Say nothing. Squeak. They will recognize the
voice of a rat.

Murray goes to the door. As he opens it Rock speaks.

ROCK. You will find cheese in the larder. Leave some
for Tom.

The door slams.

CLOSE-UP of Rock. The sardonicism, the mockery, have
vanished from his face.

DISSOLVE.

109

LONG SHOT of LONG CORRIDOR IN ROCK'S ACADEMY.

We see Tom coming up towards us from the end of the Corridor.

We see him open a door, put his head round the door. We hear
him speak into the room behind the door, but are too far away to
catch the words.

He comes on up the Corridor, opens another door, puts his head
round the door. We hear him speak into the room behind the
door, but though his voice is louder now, we still cannot catch
the words.

He comes on up the Corridor, opens the door of the Reference Library,
puts his head round the door. And now we are close enough to
hear the words.

TOM. Fallon and Broom. They've arrested Fallon and
Broom. Murder.

He withdraws his head.

From the opposite end of the Corridor we now see, in *LONG SHOT*,
Tom padding on, away from camera. . . .

DISSOLVE.

110

To another CORRIDOR.

TRACK UP the empty Corridor.

As we track we hear a mumble of voices growing louder. We reach a door marked 'Board Room.'

The noise rises.

111

INTERIOR OF BOARD ROOM.

Around the long table are attorneys, counsel, police officials, Hocking, and Green.

> FIRST POLICE OFFICIAL. . . . and if Doctor Rock did not know that these bodies were murdered, he's a far less canny gentleman than I supposed. . . .
>
> FIRST ATTORNEY. He knew. One corpse might pass him by, but Fallon and Broom were in the wholesale trade. . . .
>
> SECOND POLICE OFFICIAL. Indict him as accessory after the fact. . . .
>
> HOCKING. I do not exonerate Doctor Rock, but I will not have the whole medical profession of the City put on trial.
>
> GREEN. Accuse Rock, you accuse the integrity of all the surgeons in the City.

The Chairman (the Lord Chief Justice) nods in agreement.

> HOCKING. Oh, more than that. The whole aristocracy of learning that has been so carefully built up would be tumbled to the ground. The stain upon his character would spread across the whole of our culture. There could be no more respect for us. Indictment of Rock would mean *the death of a class.* . . .

112

PRIVATE SMOKEROOM IN AN INN (as in Sequence 27).

The two old gentlemen are seated there with silver tankards in their hands.

FIRST GENTLEMAN. A great pity his letter appeared in all the newspapers. . . .

SECOND GENTLEMAN. On the very day of the arrest. Your health!

FIRST GENTLEMAN. Health!

SECOND GENTLEMAN. It was so very untactful.

There is a silence during which they drink. They gaze at their tankards.

FIRST GENTLEMAN. 'We must have more bodies,' he said. Dear, dear.

SECOND GENTLEMAN. We must have more *murders*.

FIRST GENTLEMAN. An ugly word, Richard.

SECOND GENTLEMAN. Doctor Rock has endangered the dignity of the higher professions. . . . If he is indicted as accessory after the fact . . .

FIRST GENTLEMAN. No, no, Richard, that must never be. Guilty or not guilty, his part in this affair must be kept in a decent obscurity, or Anarchy will be walking abroad in the land. . . .

SECOND GENTLEMAN. They should all be shot against the wall. . . .

FIRST GENTLEMAN. Who, Richard?

The Second Gentleman makes a vague, sweeping gesture.

SECOND GENTLEMAN. All of 'em. . . .

113

CLOSE SHOT of two elderly professors in mortar-boards and gowns, against the background of a very large, ornately gold-framed portrait of another old professor.

FIRST PROFESSOR. I agree with you entirely. His whole attitude to society spelt ruin from the first. Attack Tradition, it always bites back; and its teeth are well grounded.

SECOND PROFESSOR. A man who could be so persistently and obnoxiously rude to his elders and intellectual betters would think *nothing* of murdering his *own children* for a penny piece.

FIRST PROFESSOR. That is, perhaps, a little extravagant. We *must* disregard personal prejudice, though I agree that to be called 'anaemic buffoon' could not predispose him in your favour. But Rock is a *symbol*. . . .

SECOND PROFESSOR. I agree. A symbol of scholarship. In a manner of speaking, we could regard ourselves as 'the royal family of the intellect,' and . . .

FIRST PROFESSOR. My dear Fraser! . . .

SECOND PROFESSOR. . . . and if a member of the royal family is accused of a commoner's crime, then it is the *whole family* that is accused. An elaborate simile—but you see my point?

And the two professors wag their chins in complete agreement.

114

INTERIOR OF BOARD ROOM.

Around the table the attorneys, counsel, police officials, Hocking, and Green.

FIRST ATTORNEY. Perhaps we are forgetting the murder of children and old women in our concern for our sacred society of autocratic schoolmen. . . .

CHAIRMAN. It is a very grave position. . . .

SECOND POLICE OFFICIAL. Rock is guilty of connivance. . . .

FIRST POLICE OFFICIAL. I am afraid we *will* have to use him as a witness, gentlemen. . . .

CHAIRMAN. Oh, certainly, certainly. . . .

The police officials rise.

CHAIRMAN. [In an undertone to Hocking next to him.] But we won't call him, of course.

115

CORRIDOR IN ROCK'S ACADEMY.

Tom padding up the Corridor.

He stops outside the Reference Library, opens the door.

From behind him we see into the library.

Rock is seated at his desk.

> TOM. Broom has turned king's evidence, sir.
>
> ROCK. [Without looking up.] The king will be pleased....

Tom closes the door, pads on up the long Corridor again, and turns a corner, leaving the Corridor empty.

We hear the very distant noise of a crowd. . . .

116

LONG SHOT of narrow CITY STREET.

Early morning.

The street is empty.

We hear, kept very low, the noise of a great crowd: the grumbling of a sea far off.

117

LONG SHOT of another narrow, empty STREET.

The noise of a great crowd rising, slowly.

118

LONG SHOT of another narrow, empty STREET.

Then, across the far end of the desolate tunnel of the street, we see the crowd surging.

And the noise increases.

The camera moves down the narrow street towards the surge of the crowd and the increasing noise.

It moves past empty doorways.

And out of the empty doorways, through the clamour of the nearing crowd, we hear chanted:

> FIRST VOICE. Up the alley and down the street . . .

On, on, past another doorway.

> SECOND VOICE. Fallon and Broom sell bones and meat....

Past another doorway.

THIRD VOICE. Fallon's the butcher, Broom's the thief . . .

Now we are nearly among the crowd pouring past the narrow street end, but we hear a fourth voice through the noise. . . .

FOURTH VOICE. And Rock's the boy who buys the beef. . . .

And now, through and under the loud noise of the crowd, we hear many voices together taking up the chant.

The camera cranes with and over the heads of the crowd and up to the windows of the court-room, and into the court-room.

119

COURT-ROOM.

We see the backs of the judges.

We move past them, across the court, towards the dock.

As we move we hear the droning voice of the Clerk of the Court. . . .

CLERK. Robert Fallon and Nelly Connor, you are both and each of you indicted and accused . . .

In the dock, facing us, are Fallon and Nelly. They are both more neatly dressed than usual. Nelly is in black. Fallon is clean-shaven.

We move past them.

Now from behind them, we look down at the Clerk of the Court, who is seated beneath the judges' bench.

The Clerk has not stopped speaking. Now the sound of his voice rises.

CLERK. . . . that albeit by the laws of this and every other well-governed realm, murder is a crime of an heinous nature, and severely punishable, yet true it is and of verity that you the said Robert Fallon and Nelly Connor are both and each, or one or other of you, guilty of the said crime. . . .

The sound of the Clerk's voice is lowered. Now it is a drone the words of which we cannot catch.

And, through the droning, we hear the muffled noise of the crowd
  outside.
We move, past Fallon and Nelly, towards the judges.
PAN ALONG the Judges' bench.
PAN DOWN to the Clerk. The Clerk's voice rises.

> CLERK. . . . when she the said Jennie Bailey was lying in
> the said house in a state of intoxication, and did, by the
> pressure thereof, and by covering her mouth and nose with
> your body or person, and forcibly compressing her throat
> with your hands, and forcibly keeping her down, notwith-
> standing her resistance, or in some other way to the prosecutor
> unknown . . .

CUT to CLOSE-UP of Fallon.

> CLERK. . . . preventing her from breathing, did suffocate or
> strangle her. . . .

The noise of the crowd rises, then is dimmed into a background.

DISSOLVE to

120

ROCK'S LECTURE HALL.

Evening.
The background of the crowd noise.
Rock is on the platform.
The candles are lit on the platform table.
The auditorium is crowded with students.
The noise of the crowd rises violently.
Through the noise of the crowd, we hear the percussive voice-beat
  of 'Rock! Rock! Rock!'
And, like a cymbal clashing, the sharp crash of smashed glass.
Stones hurl through the shattered window at one side of the Lecture
  Hall.
The students stampede to their feet.
And a heavy stone crashes at Rock's foot.

The students begin to rush down the gallery steps towards the doors
and the platform, shouting.

Rock stands rigid.

He pales with temper, glaring at the rushing students as though they
were his enemies.

In its intensity, his dignity is malevolent.

      ROCK. Gentlemen!

Cold, controlled fury stops the rush.

The students stand frozen.

The noise of the crowd is still loud.

> ROCK. I have attempted to teach you the dignity of man;
> I have succeeded in producing the degradation of a *mob*.
> Because the verminous gutter-snipes of the City snarl and
> gibber in the street, because the scum from the brothels and
> the rot-gut shops howl for blood outside my window, must
> *you* conduct yourselves, in return, as though you were born
> in a quagmire and nurtured on hog-wash?
>
> Take your seats. Pay no attention to *the mob*. The mob
> can never win. Remember that the louder a man shouts,
> the emptier is his argument.
>
> Remember that you are here to study osteology, syndes-
> mology, myology, angiology, neurology, splanchnology:
> not bar-room pugilism or the morals of the crapulous bog-
> trotter and the tosspot.
>
> [In his usual lecturing voice.] The heart, gentlemen, is
> a four-chambered muscular bag which lies in the cavity
> of the thorax . . .

DISSOLVE to

121

CITY STREET.

Night.

The noise of the crowd is a distant, insistent background. We see,
striding in front of us, the black-cloaked top-hatted figure of
Rock with his heavy stick.

We follow him along the street.

Two figures, muffled against the cold, come out of a side-street.

They stumble into Rock.

He pushes them aside.

And suddenly one of them cries out:

> FIRST MAN. Rock! Rock! Doctor Rock!

Rock strides on.

The men cry after him, and follow him down the street, though keeping a safe distance from him.

> SECOND MAN. Doctor Rock! Rock!

And, from some way off, we hear the crowd take up the percussive noise of 'Rock! Rock! Rock!'

122

DISSOLVE to Rock, hatless, but still in his cloak, entering ELIZABETH'S ROOM.

Elizabeth, by the fire, is sewing.

Elizabeth looks up as he comes in, and puts her sewing down.

He crosses to her; kisses her; stands still then, looking down at her.

CLOSE-UP of Rock and Elizabeth.

> ROCK. Oh, there's peace in here.
>
> ELIZABETH. You didn't come home *alone* through the streets? I've been hearing the crowd everywhere, all the evening.
>
> ROCK. Alone.
>
> ELIZABETH. They might have hurt you. . . .
>
> ROCK. Hurt *me*?

With a flourish he opens his cloak. Stuck in a belt around his waist are two pistols and a long dagger.

> ROCK. I'd fell them to the ground. I'd flood the gutters with their . . .

Elizabeth begins to laugh, though quite gently.

> ELIZABETH. Take off your cloak. And put your silly knives and guns away. You're like a boy pretending to be a

highwayman. 'Stand and deliver.' Oh, Thomas, my dear . . .

He takes off his cloak and flings it over a chair and places the belt, the knife, and the guns on a table near the fire: a small table covered with sewing and bales of wool and cotton reels.

ELIZABETH. Why do you have to go out alone at night, *now*? Why do you *always* have to be alone?

ROCK. If the crowd wants me, it can have me. I am not going to hide. I am not going to surround myself by a company of paid protectors. . . .

ELIZABETH. [Softly.] I've always wanted to see another country. Couldn't we go away? Every one is against us here, now.

The distant noise of the crowd.

ELIZABETH. The women in the street didn't nod to me this morning. Not because I'm your wife—that's why they used to have nothing to do with me—but because *you*'re my husband.

ROCK. We won't go away.

ELIZABETH. [Gently, as throughout.] I know why. You want to show them that they can't hurt you by calling you names. You want to show them that you don't *mind* when they say that you told those men to murder people. But they *do* hurt you.

ROCK. *Time's a wilderness.* [Then, in a changed voice.] Do you remember walking in the park? Oh, not so long ago. It was very, very, very cold and windy, people were scudding along like ships in a gale, and I remember thinking: 'Here's my life going true and even, and my children growing, and Elizabeth with me for ever, and books to write, and work to do. . . . Lord, but it's a happy time . . . even in the unhappy times.'

ELIZABETH. I'm with you for ever, that's true. And there's books to write, and work to do.

Noise of the crowd nearer.

ROCK. [Suddenly in another mood.] I was successful, I was established, I was standing in the light. . . . Then out of the mud of the darkness come two ignorant animals, and slowly, quite unknown to themselves, they set about the task of bringing my life and my work down, down, into the slime that bred them. . . . Perhaps from the very moment of their monstrous births, it was decreed, by some sadistic jack-in-office of the universe, that they should befoul and ruin a fellow creature they had never heard of: a garrulous, over-credulous, conceited little anatomist, in a city they had never seen. . . .

From outside the noise of the crowd rises. And as the noise rises, so the voices of Elizabeth and Rock become quieter and more intimate.

ELIZABETH. Let us go away.

ROCK. No, we must stay for ever.

ELIZABETH. I have never asked you before, Thomas, because I love you. Did you know that the bodies that those men brought you had been murdered?

The noise of the crowd rises. Now it is very loud.

And the night sky beyond the window is glowing.

Elizabeth and Rock turn sharply to look towards the window.

VOICES OF THE CROWD. Rock! Rock!
Hang Rock!
Burn him!
Burn!
Burn!
Rock's the boy who buys the beef. . . .

Annabella comes in. She is palely, composedly angry.

ANNABELLA. Do you know what those hooligans are *doing*, Thomas?

She crosses to the window.

ROCK. I gather that they are not subscribing to a testimonial to me. . . .

ANNABELLA. Look! Look!

She points accusingly out of the window.

And Rock and Elizabeth, he with his arm around her shoulder, cross to Annabella's side and look, through the window, down on to the street.

123

STREET OUTSIDE ROCK'S HOUSE.

We see, from the window, the crowd straining against the iron railings of the house; the crowd, in the middle of the street, dancing with torches in their hands; the crowd carrying an effigy of Rock, an absurdly top-hatted scarecrow; the crowd waving their torches, stamping, howling, making a witches' Sabbath in the decorous, graciously façaded street.

And then the effigy, the guy carried on a pole, is held in a position directly opposite the window.

And a young woman with wild hair thrusts her blazing torch into the belly of the effigy.

In the torchlight, in the light of the burning Rock, we see that the young woman is Alice.

And another torch is thrust into the burning body; and another; and another.

Soon the effigy is writhing on fire. And the crowd waves it, crying in a high, hysterical triumph.

And they carry it along the street; and the dark figures of the crowd, their torches above them like long streams of fiery hair, follow it down the street.

124

CITY SQUARE.

Night.

Outside Rock's Academy stand Murray and Tom.

Crowd noise, in the not so far distance.

> MURRAY. What's the light over there?

The sky beyond the Square is glowing.

TOM. They're burning an auld scarecrow of the Doctor in the streets.

CLOSE SHOT of Murray. He says, softly:

MURRAY. Can that children's magic bring back the dead?

The crowd noise rises on the wind.

MURRAY. Here we are, Tom, the two of us: the two 'rats'! the two 'deserters'!

TOM. Aye, the Doctor was wrong again. We're no 'rats' or 'deserters.' He should have known we didna want to lose our jobs, eh, Mr. Murray?

Murray draws a little way apart from Tom, then asks abruptly:

MURRAY. What's the time?

TOM. One after midnight. The trial's been nearly twelve hours now. . . .

CLOSE SHOT of Murray.

MURRAY. It took a few short minutes to stop her breath. . . .

125

COURT-ROOM.

Broom in the witness-box.

We see him very close.

We hear the Prosecutor, but do not see him.

PROSECUTOR'S VOICE. What did he do then?

BROOM. He got on her with his breast on her head, and kept in her breath; she gave a kind of cry and moaned a little after the first cry. . . .

CUT to *CLOSE-UP* of Fallon in the dock.

PROSECUTOR'S VOICE. Did he say anything while this was going on?

BROOM'S VOICE. No, he got up then and put his hand across her mouth and kept it there three or four minutes. She appeared quite dead then.

PROSECUTOR'S VOICE. Were you looking on all this while?

CUT to *CLOSE-UP* of Broom.

> BROOM. I was sittin' on the chair.
> PROSECUTOR'S VOICE. Did you sit in that chair and see Fallon for ten minutes killing the woman, and offer her no assistance?
> BROOM. Aye.

Broom smiles.

126

NEWSPAPER OFFICE.

Crowd noise from outside.
A room with a long, large window.
The First Reporter is writing at a table.
The Second Reporter is walking up and down the room and glancing, every few moments, out of the window.

> SECOND REPORTER. Was he smiling when he said *that*?
> FIRST REPORTER. [Without looking up.] If you call it smiling.
> SECOND REPORTER. What did he look like?
> FIRST REPORTER. [Briefly, as he writes.] Devil.
> SECOND REPORTER. Fallon?
> FIRST REPORTER. Quite quiet. Vurry polite.
> SECOND REPORTER. And the woman?
> FIRST REPORTER. Sober.

The crowd noise rises.

> SECOND REPORTER. What are you calling the article? [At the window.] They're running down the street now. . . Thousands of them. . . .
> FIRST REPORTER. 'Justice.'
> SECOND REPORTER. 'Broom! Broom! Broom!' . . . D' you hear them?
> FIRST REPORTER. Broom 'll go free.
> SECOND REPORTER. [Still looking out of the window.]

There s another fire over Newington way . . . somewhere near Rock's place. . . . D' you hear them?

FIRST REPORTER. [Writing, not looking up.] They won't call Rock as a witness. That'll be taken care of. . . .

A great cry from the crowd outside. . . .

SECOND REPORTER. D' you hear that? . . .

FIRST REPORTER. I'm not deaf. They're nearing the end now. . . .

127

COURT-ROOM.

CLOSE SHOT of Lord Meadowbank. Camera *PANS ALONG* judges' faces.

LORD MEADOWBANK. My Lords, I am confident that, although speaking in the presence of your Lordships, so much better instructed than myself, and so able to correct me were I in error, there is no chance of my being contra-dicted when I say that in the history of this country—nay, in the whole history of civilized society—there has never been exhibited such a system of barbarous and savage iniquity, or anything at all corresponding in atrocity, to what this trial has brought to light. . . .

128

NEWSPAPER OFFICE.

Night.

The two reporters.

The First Reporter flings down his pen.

FIRST REPORTER. Fallon guilty. The rest—innocent! And my title is 'Justice.' I wrote the verdict *myself*, hours ago. Only the sentence now: I've written that, too.

129

COURT-ROOM.

LORD CHIEF JUSTICE. The Lord Justice Clerk and Lord Commissioners of Justiciary in respect of the verdict before recorded, determine and adjudge the said Robert Fallon, to be carried from the bar, and to be fed upon bread and water only until Wednesday, the 28th January, and upon that day to be taken forth to the common place of execution and then and there between the hours of eight and ten o'clock to be hanged by the neck until he be dead. And may Almighty God have mercy on your soul.

DISSOLVE to

130

Large *CLOSE-UP* of Rock.

ROCK. I have no need of your sympathy. When I see a tear, I smell a crocodile.

TRACK BACK to show that Rock is standing on the platform of the empty Lecture Hall. Murray, a good distance from Rock, stands at the window, looking out.

Their voices echo in the Hall.

MURRAY. [Turning round.] For God's sake, Thomas, can you do nothing but—stand still and gibe?

ROCK. Would you have me death-dance and *moan*, like a Gaelic dipsomaniac at a distillery fire? Must tragedy go immediately to the feet and the tongue? Because I can observe my history *calmly* as it burns and topples around me, you emotional gluttons think yourselves cheated. 'Oh, he can't *feel* anything,' you say. 'When we told him his life was over, he did not tear the relics of his hair or address the travelling moon in blank verse. He blew his nose and called for Burgundy.'

MURRAY. [Deliberately.] Fallon is to hang.

ROCK. A quick end. If they wished his death to be longer

and infinitely more painful, they should marry him to Doctor Hocking's daughter.

MURRAY. Fallon is to hang. Nelly Connor is 'not guilty'! Broom and his woman are free to murder again! And *you*?

ROCK. I shall stay here.

I shall listen to the voices of the crowd outside my window, *inside my head*; it will not be long before they forget me; I shall never forget them.

I shall stay here. The whispers of the slanderer and the backbiter will always be with me: mice behind the wall.

I shall stay here. I shall count my friends on the fingers of one hand, then on one finger, then on none.

Camera Cranes Back, looking down at Rock and Murray all the time, over the empty tiers of the classroom.

Although Rock becomes further and further off, in *LONG SHOT*, the sound, booming hollowly through the empty classroom, remains in full close-up.

ROCK. My lectures will be very well attended, at the beginning. I shall possess a sinister attraction to the young: dangerous and exciting, like dining with a vampire. But the attendance will diminish.

I shall stay here to see in the eyes of the passing stranger in the street cruelty and contempt; in the eyes of the poor the terrible accusation: 'You killed the lost, the weak, the homeless, the hopeless, the helpless. Murderer of the poor!'

God help me, life will go on. . . .

131

CONDEMNED CELL.

Fallon on a chair in the middle of the cell.

His hair is shaven.

A Phrenologist is measuring his head. He speaks the measurements aloud to an assistant, who writes them down in a book.

Fallon submits, with interest, to the examination.

PHRENOLOGIST. From the ear to lower Individuality: 5 inches.
From the ear to the centre of philo-progenitiveness: 4·8.
From the ear to Benevolence: 5·7. From . the ear to
Destructiveness: 6·125.

Let us see:

Acquisitiveness: large.

Secretiveness: large.

Wit: deficient.

Cautiousness: h'm, rather large.

Sense of Tune: moderate.

Self-esteem: rather large.

Hope: small.

132

EXTERIOR OF PRISON.

Night.

A coach draws up.

The driver is heavily shawled about, and his hat is pulled down
over his eyes.

And two cloaked, muffled figures hurry Broom towards the coach.

Broom is wrapped in a thick coat, and hooded. It is hard to
recognize him.

But suddenly, at the door of the coach, he pulls back his hood,
looks up at the sky.

He shakes his shaven head, like a monstrous dog coming out of the
water.

And he begins to laugh his high, clear, yelping laugh as the two
cloaked figures smuggle him into the coach.

The coach moves off, out of picture.

133

MARKET-PLACE.

Late evening.

The stalls closed down.

And a woman's scream, a scream of hate and anger, is coming
from a Market tavern.

And with her scream are mingled the voices of men and women: voices shouting, cursing, and threatening.

Then a knot of people tangles inside the open door of the tavern.

A whirl of arms and a squall of voices.

And we see Kate thrown out of the tavern on to the cobble stones of the Market.

She stumbles to her feet, runs, squawking like a chased hen, down the Market.

But only the voices chase her.

People pour from the tavern, stand outside it, throw stones after her, manure, rubbish.

Kate runs on, huddled.

And windows, high up in the tenements around the Market, open.

And the contents of buckets are thrown upon her as she runs.

134

ROAD ON THE OUTSKIRTS OF THE CITY.

Night.

The road is long and winding.

We see Nelly Connor, with a bundle on her back, coming towards us, along the road, out of the distance.

She is pushing a hurly: a hurly with old boots upon it, and remnants of clothing, and odds and ends from the room in Rag-and-Bone Alley, and shapes one cannot identify in the night.

And we hear her voice as she pushes her barrow through darkness up the desolate road that leads out of the City.

    NELLY's VOICE. [Softly.]
      Old boots to sell! . . . Cat-skin! . . . *Human hair!* . . .

135

NEWSPAPER OFFICE.

Daylight.

We see the street through the tall window.

The Second Reporter stands at the window, looking out, his back towards us.

The First Reporter sits at the other side of the window, a pad on his knee. Through the window we see, at the end of the street, in *LONG SHOT*, a scaffold.

The platform of the scaffold is raised above the heads of the crowd.

On the platform we see the gibbet; it is shaped like a T with one additional vertical on the right.

On the platform are several figures: clergymen, magistrates, hangman, and Fallon.

And we hear the crowd noise rise.

And looking through the window at the scene of execution, and hearing the cries of the crowd, we hear, too, the voices of the two men at the window.

> SECOND REPORTER. Do you hear?
> 'Hang Broom! Hang Rock!'
> FIRST REPORTER. Fallon's on his knees. He's praying.

The noise of the crowd rises. Then:

> SECOND REPORTER. The rope's round his neck. They've put a cotton nightcap on his head.
> FIRST REPORTER. Good night.

The noise of the crowd rises again.

> CRIES OF THE CROWD. You'll see Billy Bedlam in a minute.
> FIRST REPORTER. What are they shouting?
> SECOND REPORTER. 'You'll see Billy Bedlam in a minute!' He's on the drop.

A great cheer from the crowd.

> FIRST REPORTER. He was always one for dancing. He's dancing now.

136

CLOSE SHOT of Alice and Murray at a table in a TAVERN.

Around them the noise of the Market-place drinking. And pipes in the distance.

> ALICE. Fallon's dead—why isn't the Doctor dead? Nobody remembers Jennie now.
>
> MURRAY. Oh, there's lots of ways of dying. *I* remember.

137

CLOSE SHOT of Annabella and Elizabeth; behind them, the window of ELIZABETH'S ROOM looking out on the wintry trees in the garden.

> ANNABELLA. Do you *know* what it is to be lonely? I've always been lonely. I wanted to be mistress of my brother's house, I wanted to give dinner parties and dances and be charming and admired. I wanted to marry. But people wouldn't visit us because *you* married *him*. It doesn't matter now. Now nobody 'll come. . . .
>
> ELIZABETH. I married him because I loved him. But we're only a very little part of his life, Bella.
>
> I've been lonely, too.

138

CLOSE SHOT of Hocking and the Chairman (the Lord Chief Justice, whom we saw in Sequences 111 and 114) against the background of imposing bookcases.

> CHAIRMAN. So, officially speaking, he's innocent as a lamb, the wolf.
>
> HOCKING. We saved him from a criminal prosecution.
>
> CHAIRMAN. Of course, of course. In order to save the good name of society. Fallon and Broom could have brought

their bodies to *you*, of course. It just happened it was Rock they chose.

HOCKING. I would have none of their bodies.

CHAIRMAN. No?

HOCKING. But now it's all over. All over. We can speak our minds now.

CHAIRMAN. We save him from public ruin, so that we can ruin him privately. H'm, I'm sure he's grateful. . . .

139

LECTURE HALL OF ROCK'S ACADEMY.

Rock is on the platform.

The auditorium is densely packed.

We see Rock from the back of the Hall, over the heads of the students.

And we move, slowly, over the heads towards him as he speaks.

ROCK. To think, then, is to enter into a perilous country, colder of welcome than the polar wastes, darker than a Scottish Sunday, where the hand of the unthinker is always raised against you, where the wild animals, who go by such names as Envy, Hypocrisy, and Tradition, are notoriously carnivorous, and *where the parasites rule.*

To *think* is dangerous. The majority of men have found it easier to writhe their way into the parasitical bureaucracy, or to *droop* into the slack ranks of the ruled. I beg you all to devote your lives to danger; I pledge you to adventure; I command you to experiment. [Slowly.] Remember that the practice of Anatomy is absolutely vital to the *progress* of medicine. Remember that the progress of medicine is vital to the progress of mankind. And mankind is worth fighting for: killing and lying and dying for. Forget what you like. Forget all I have ever told you. But remember that. . . .

Now we see Rock in CLOSE-UP.

DISSOLVE to

140

CITY STREET.

Gathering dusk.

We hear the thin, high singing of the wind in the street.

And, in the background, the sound of the voices of children drifting through the dusk.

Rock, from a grey distance, is walking towards us along the street. He is cloaked, top-hatted.

And as he comes closer to us a little girl runs out of the shadows of a side-street, runs barefoot through the wind, her black hair leaping.

She is grimed from the gutters of the city; her dress is thin and ragged; one shoulder is naked.

And she runs at Rock's side, crying out:

> GIRL. Give us a penny, mister, give us a penny. . . .

The camera *TRACKS BACK* as Rock, and the little girl running at his side, move on down the street.

Then Rock stops, at a corner.

And the little girl stops; she stands still in a shadow at the mouth of a narrow tunnel-like street. She is almost lost in the shadow, her hair is mixed into the darkness, but we see her white face and white, naked shoulder.

Rock stands just outside the shadow.

He puts a penny in her hand.

He looks down at her, and is silent for a moment.

> ROCK. It's a bitter cold night to be running about in the streets. You should go home.

The child in the shadows shakes her head.

> CHILD. Granny says I can't come home till I got four-pence. . . .

Rock fumbles in his pocket for another coin.

The child holds out her hand from the shadow around her.

Rock. What's your name, lassie?

Child. I'm Maggie Bell.

Rock. [Almost as though to himself.] I'm Doctor Rock.

And the child runs screaming into the darkness.

And Rock walks on, away from us.

141

HILL ABOVE THE CITY.

The dusk is deeper. . . .

The wind is blowing wilder. . . .

We look down the hill.

Out of the dusk, a long way off, Rock is climbing up towards us.

And as he climbs, we hear his voice.   But it is only the little, wind-blown whisper of a voice, and we cannot hear a word of it.

And as he climbs on and up, so the windy whisper loudens and we begin to hear the words.

We begin to hear the fragments of sentences.

We hear some words and then the wind rises for a second and blows them away.

Then we hear more words, from the voice of his mind; the wind again will not let the words finish but blows them away.

And again; and again; and again.

Always the voice is the voice of Rock, but it is never twice on the same level: it is the voice of Rock young, then old, then gay, then sad; a high voice, a low voice.

And the sound of it rises as he climbs.

Rock's Voice.   And the child in the cold runs away from my name. . . .

My name is a ghost to frighten children. . . .

Will *my* children cry 'Murder' and 'Blood' when I touch them . . . as if my hands were Fallon's hands? . . .

'Be good, be good, or the terrible Doctor will come with his knife.'

133

Poor Billy! I came to you with my knife.

Did I *know*, did I *know* from the very beginning?

Never answer, never answer, even to yourself alone in
the night. . . .

All's over now. . . .

Oh, Elizabeth, hold my hand. . . .

'Oh, it isn't a hand, it's a pair of scissors! . . .'

Did I set myself up as a little god over death?

Over death. . . .

All over . . . over . . . over . . .

Did I set myself above pity? . . .

Oh, my God, I knew what I was doing!

And he passes us and climbs up the long hill, and his voice climbs
with him into darkness, into a whisper, into silence, into the
climax of

MUSIC.

THE STORY OF THE FILM

BY DONALD TAYLOR

Since the film has attained a certain intellectual maturity in the half-century since its birth, the publication of screenplays has become increasingly frequent. Hitherto those screenplays which achieve the dignity of print have been verbal transcriptions taken from the finished film, when that film has been successful in the cinemas. It is what is known in the film industry as a 'release script.'

It is worth recording that in the majority of cases, the finished film is very different from the original screenplay as delivered by the script writer. It would be infinitely more instructive to the layman were there to be a comparative publication of the original screenplay alongside a transcription of the finished product. The transcription method does not reveal the essential factor about film-making, which is the varied contributions made by many hands and the constant polishing and alteration that is the integral part of the work.

Even the great Eisenstein was not above attempting to demonstrate his creative competence by publishing graphs of sequences from his films to prove his creative planning; which to the film technician are only too evidently the result of trial and error.

The screenplay of *The Doctor and the Devils* is the first to be published as a book before the film has been produced. This is no doubt due to the literary quality, unusual in this medium. It will be instructive to compare the finished film, when it is produced, with this screenplay.

The most satisfying and commercially successful films have a background of idea which is the driving force behind the plot. The classic example is D. W. Griffith's *Intolerance*. It is insufficient in making any film to have a good plot, if there is no basic motive behind it.

The screenplay of *The Doctor and the Devils* was written because I had been searching for some years to find a story that would pose the question of 'the ends justifying the means.'

Concurrently with this, I had been much interested in James Bridie's play *The Anatomist*. This prompted me to do some research into the character of Dr. Knox, the Edinburgh anatomist of the early nineteenth century. The question of whether he was aware that the bodies supplied to him by two Irish labourers Burke and Hare, for anatomical research and demonstration, were the product of mass murder, seemed to me an interesting basis to illustrate my theme. Contemporary and historical records seemed to assume a verdict of not proven; although Professor Wilson, the brilliant and caustic Edinburgh philosopher, declared in his *Noctes Ambrosianae* that Knox should have been hanged with Burke and Hare. We found such a wealth of material about Dr. Knox that, for all of us who worked on the subject, the study of the man became all absorbing. From this material I organized and wrote a coherent story and commissioned Dylan Thomas, who was then working for me, to write a screen play.

It is surely time that a considered biography was written about Knox, who contributed so much to British anatomical science and was known in his time as a great European figure. The only bio-graphy, published in 1870 and never reprinted, was written by his senior demonstrator, who subsequently became Surgeon Extraordinary to Queen Victoria. It is a testament to Dr. Knox's ability as scientist, anatomist, and lecturer, that his chief pupil should have written so glowing a biography thirty years after his death.

The limitations of the film medium are such that one must express a character through a very short series of incidents and these must form a fairly rigid pattern. This means that much that is interesting and significant has to be ruthlessly cut out. For instance, by one of those historical coincidences which seems incredible, Knox was a doctor at Waterloo when Burke, who was subsequently to change the whole pattern of his life, acted as medical orderly in the same battle.

What is in this script is in fact true, although to achieve dramatic construction many of the incidents have had to be telescoped and concentrated. The names of the characters have been changed to

136

conform with film censorship. The only 'invented' individual, who did in fact exist but invented in the sense of character, is the wife of Knox. His biographer makes only two references to her, both of which are significant. At one point he says that Knox 'married beneath him' and the second that 'when she died, he threw himself upon her grave and lay there for hours together.' These two facts made possible a character of charm in a gloomy picture.

Dr. Knox was an odd and eccentric being; he was a man of insignificant height, bald, and with one eye. At the height of his success his anatomical lectures drew not only all the students from the university, but famous people from all over Europe. He was always overdressed and in the height of fashion; the amount of jewellery he wore caused remark among his contemporaries. But he had only to walk in front of his audience to hold them completely under his sway for two or three hours at a time. His lectures, although inspired by an anatomical text, ranged through the whole world of philosophy, art, and manners. He was a man of such diverse attainments that it is hard to conceive that he could ever have achieved so much in the relatively short period when he was famous.

He was at Waterloo as a newly qualified doctor; he was a pioneer and road builder in the development of the Boer States, with such success that he was invited by the Boers to become a member of their legislative assembly; he sat under Cuvier and was much respected by him; he contributed a scientific approach to ethnographical study; he was an indefatigable fisherman and discovered a new species of fish that inhabited Loch Maben; he was a continuous correspondent to every medical journal of his time, and he was a confirmed and distinguished controversialist in newspapers and literary reviews; he contributed much to scientific study and speculation outside his own specialized work in anatomy.

It is a sad fact that so remarkable a man is only remembered to-day because his name is linked with two murderers. This trial ruined his Edinburgh career.

It is ironic that the present acts of Parliament which secure the supply of bodies for anatomical study, should have resulted from the trial of Burke and Hare. Knox was never brought to trial,

137

because the Edinburgh aristocracy of intellect considered that were he to be prosecuted, the intellectual leadership of Scotland that had been so effectively built up to replace the aristocratic leadership destroyed by the rising of '45, could not survive the public arraignment of one of their members.

After the trial of Burke and Hare, Knox was ostracized by Edinburgh society; in the heat of the moment after the trial he was in daily danger of his life from the mob. Although he tried to brave it out, he had eventually to leave Edinburgh, and his detractors claimed that he was last seen lecturing in a circus in Leicester Square, London. The real fact is that ethnography, his abiding passion, led him to lecture to invited audiences, using for demonstration purposes a group of North American Indians who were appearing in a circus.

Although he had many a brush with poverty in his later years, he achieved some measure of security and fame in London. He remained to the end a vigorous correspondent and controversialist, and, whatever Edinburgh society might think, the medical world of London respected him sufficiently to appoint him the first surgeon to the new London Fever Hospital.

I must acknowledge contributions made by members of my film unit, the Strand Film Company, and I must record my grateful thanks to Mr. Earl St. John and the J. Arthur Rank organization for allowing me to publish this work.

D. T.

1953.

A Film Script of

TWENTY YEARS A-GROWING

by

Dylan Thomas

from the story by

Maurice O'Sullivan

'Here is the egg of a seabird—lovely, perfect and laid this very morning.' So wrote E. M. Forster when *Twenty Years A-Growing* by Maurice O'Sullivan was first published in English in 1933. In his unfinished film script of the first half of the book, Dylan Thomas has preserved this freshness. The script has only recently come to light, and becomes a new creation in the lovely and evocative style of its author.

*   *   *   *

The Blasket Islands lie off the Kerry Coast in the extreme south-west corner of Ireland. They are now uninhabited except for occasional summer-time holiday-makers. The district is still Irish-speaking.

It is morning in the market-town of Dingle. A cracked school bell is ringing. The main street is wide awake: a man leans at a corner, motionless, smoking. A woman stands at an open doorway, looking at the morning. A large pig crosses the road slowly, and enters a cottage. The school bell still rings.

Then, at the top of the street, appear a countrywoman and a little boy in a smock, hand in hand. They walk on down the street towards us.

And suddenly we hear a crying and shouting, and there appear, at the top of the street and behind the woman and the little boy, a helter-skelter of children who run down towards us. And as they run, so other children come out of the cottages, on either side of the street, and join them. And they all scamper past the woman and the little boy, making quite a noise, and past us and out of the picture.

And as the woman and the little boy approach us now, hand in hand, the little boy clinging, we hear the voice of Maurice O'Sullivan the man, gently, reminiscently talking, as a person to no audience but himself and a friend.

THE VOICE. And that's indeed the first thing I remember very clearly in all my life. It was in the town of Dingle, County Kerry, Ireland, and I was going on my first day to school, holding the hand of Peg de Roiste. For it was she who took care of me when my mother died, dear God bless her soul and the souls of all the dead. Faith, there in my memory still I see old Peg and myself, Maurice O'Sullivan, walking to school.

And Peg de Roiste and little Maurice O'Sullivan are walking now towards the entrance of the whitewashed village school. The cracked bell stops ringing. He clings hard to her hand, and looks up at her, and she smiles down, nodding and reassuring, as they go into the school.

Now we are in the schoolroom: a whitewashed room with rows of benches full of children and a little chair and table at the end, and a blackboard.   At the end of the room, behind the table, stand two posts coming down from the roof to the floor.   Peg de Roiste and Maurice sit close together on the back bench.   He stares around the classroom, quiet as a mouse, his eyes wide.   All the other children are making a power of noise.

The schoolmistress enters.

The noise is hushed.

THE CHILDREN. Good morning, mistress.

The schoolmistress sits at her table, opens a book, looks at the children, marks down their names, silently. . . .

THE VOICE. I remember there was teaching us as schoolmistress a woman who was grey as a badger, with two tusks of teeth hanging down over her lip, and if she wasn't cross, it isn't day yet.   She was the devil itself, or so I thought.

Close now to Peg and Maurice: we hear him whisper timidly.

MAURICE. Where are the nice sweets you said there'd be, Peg?

PEG. Go up now, she's for giving you the sweets.

Maurice shakes his head and clings harder to her hand. And Peg gets up with him and takes him by the hand to the little table.

From the back of the classroom now we see the backs of Peg and Maurice and the face of the schoolmistress.

MISTRESS. Who are you and what is your name?

MAURICE. They call me Maurice.

MISTRESS. Maurice what?

MAURICE. Maurice.

We hear Peg whisper to the mistress, who nods and writes in her book.

Then the mistress rises and goes to a cupboard and takes out a big tin of sweets and puts it on the little table before Maurice.

We *TRACK UP* towards the table.   Maurice timidly puts his hand into the tin and takes out a sweet in the shape of a horse.

MAURICE (with wonder). A horse.

142

The mistress nods.

He puts his hand in again and takes out another-shaped sweet.

MAURICE (a little louder). A boat.

She nods.

He dips and takes out another two sweets, one in each hand. He
raises his hands to show Peg.

MAURICE (shrill with excitement). Oh, a man. And a pig.

MISTRESS. Be a good boy now and go back to the bench. And
come to school every day.

MAURICE. I *will*.

Holding his treasures, he goes to the back bench.

MISTRESS. You will, surely.

And Peg goes past him, and touches his hand, and is gone.

And we see Maurice close, as he sits in contentment, sucking the
sweet horse, and the children in unison begin to recite their morning lesson.

DISSOLVE to

The children in the playground, kicking a football. Maurice
among them. The football strikes him on the head, and bounces
off. The others go on playing, but Maurice, standing alone, lifts
up his head to the sky and howls, like a child alone in the world.

DISSOLVE to

Dingle main street, at morning again, with the cracked bell ringing.
And down the street, scattering the chickens, come the noisy children, Maurice among them.

CUT to

The classroom. Maurice is now sitting on a bench in the middle, a
little boy next to him who is Mickil Dick.

All the children are repeating a lesson. And through their voices
and the voice of Maurice we hear:

THE VOICE. I was going to school every day, growing older and bigger and none the wiser at all, I am guessing, and it was the gentleness and the sweets had long grown cold. It seemed to me there was nobody in the world had a worse life than myself. I did not know what I wanted, but I knew it was not to be kept indoors all day, like a baby or a girl. I wanted to be, oh, I knew not where . . .

And we see, as the Voice speaks, that Maurice is not joining in the speaking-aloud of the lesson but is lost in a world of his own mazy making. Suddenly the mistress's voice cuts across the voices of the children, and they stop.

MISTRESS'S VOICE. Maurice O'Sullivan.

He raises his eyes. We do not see the mistress, but only, close, the benches of children.

MISTRESS'S VOICE. You are dreaming again. Come here.

Maurice rises and crosses out of the picture.

MISTRESS'S VOICE. Put out your hand.

We see the intent faces of the children staring at the invisible punishment. One child nudges another, smiling. But most are dead quiet. We hear the sound of a stinging slap.
Mickil, next to Maurice's empty place on the bench, winces and involuntarily draws back his hand.
Another stinging slap.
Mickil's face is set and white.
Another slap.
Maurice returns; takes his place; sits stiffly, staring in front of him with very bright eyes.
And the children begin to recite together again.
Maurice moves his lips. We hear very softly, through the voices of the children, the voice of the child Maurice.

MAURICE. Your soul to the devil, you old herring. . . .

Now Maurice is coming out of a Dingle cottage—a cottage not in the main street we have seen before but in a country road. He carries his school-books hung over his shoulder. With him is Mickil. And once more the cracked school bell is ringing, but farther off than before.

They dawdle down the road together, their school-books swinging, slashing off the tops of the roadside ferns, idly kicking the stones.

MAURICE. I don't know why in the world we are going to school, on a day like this, Mickil.

MICKIL. We could be having the day under the hedge . . .

MAURICE. We could be playing the devil up on the Hill of the Cairn, or making shapes out of sticks . . .

MICKIL. Or snatching the bags of sugar out of the hands of the old men in the poor-house . . .

MAURICE. Or dabbling in the boghole, by God. . . . Oh, when will I be a grown man, Mickil, with a pony and cart and a clay pipe maybe. . . . Whisht! Who's that there?

Up the road towards them come two women and a man. They wave at Maurice and Mickil and walk on straight towards them. Maurice turns and runs in the other direction, and hides in the hedge.

From the hedge we see what he sees: the man and the women talking to Mickil and pointing up, smiling, towards the hedge. One of the women puts an orange in Mickil's hand, and the other woman gropes in her bag for a present. And, still from the hedge, we see Maurice run back towards them, stopping shyly a yard away.

WOMAN. Why did you run away just now?

MAURICE (bashfully). Nothing. . . .

WOMAN. Do you know who I am?

MAURICE. I do not.

WOMAN. I am your aunt, my treasure.

She takes Maurice up in her arms and kisses him, then puts him down again but holds him close to her.

And the other woman kisses him also.

WOMAN. That is another aunt, too, and this is your uncle.
MAN. (An elaborate greeting in Irish.)

The school bell stops ringing.

MAURICE. What sort of talk has that man?
WOMAN. That's Irish.
MAURICE. What's Irish?
WOMAN. Oh, wait now till you go home, that is the time you will
have the Irish.
MAURICE. Where is my home? We have no Irish at all in this
home here.
WOMAN. This is not your home, Maurice. Your home is in the
Blasket.

Maurice looks, without understanding, at the faces of his aunts and
his uncle.

MAN. (A speech in Irish.)

And the speech is softened so that, through it, we hear:

THE VOICE (softly). But I was as blind to what he was saying about
the Blasket as the herring leaping in the Bay of Dingle . . .
MAURICE (to the woman, who still holds him close). What is the
Blasket?
WOMAN. It is an island.
MAURICE. Is it a long way away? Over the sea?
WOMAN. It is ten miles from Dingle . . .
MICKIL. Ten miles, God be with us . . .
FIRST WOMAN. Oh, hear him. You were born on the Blasket,
Maurice, asthore, and because you were only half a year old when
your mother died . . .
SECOND WOMAN. Dear God bless her soul and the souls of all the
dead . . .
FIRST WOMAN. . . . your father sent you to Dingle to be cared for by
Peg de Roiste. Has she never been telling you that? . . .

146

WOMAN. And your father is for coming out before long to take you home at last. Would you like that, Maurice?

MAURICE. Who is my father?

WOMAN. Isn't it often your father was talking to you? You should have known him long ago . . .

MAURICE. I don't know which of the men he is, for many come . . .

WOMAN. Oh musha, youth is a queer thing. . . .

And the women give Maurice and Mickil sweets, apples and oranges.

And the man comes up to them both, and, talking Irish, solemnly shakes their hands. As he talks, Maurice and Mickil look at one another in wonder. Then he takes money from his pocket and gives Maurice a half a crown and Mickil a shilling . . .

And the two aunts kiss Maurice again.

FIRST WOMAN. Now we go to see Peg de Roiste. Farewell, and a blessing (in Irish).

SECOND WOMAN. Farewell, and a blessing (in Irish).

MAN. Farewell, and a blessing (in Irish).

And they go up the road.

CLOSE-UP of Maurice and Mickil. Mickil outs his shilling for Maurice to see.

MICKIL. I never saw a penny as bright as that. . . . Where is yours?

MAURICE. Look, mine is bigger.

MICKIL. I don't know what we had better buy with them . . .

MAURICE. Marbles and boats and . . . Oh, Mickil, the bell has stopped!

And they race down the road.

The classroom.

The mistress is chalking on the blackboard, her back to the children.

The door creaks open and Maurice and Mickil creep in to their places on the bench.

They look up fearfully at the blackboard and the mistress, who has not turned round.

Under the words of the lesson chalked on the blackboard, she writes:

Maurice and Mickil are an hour late.

The two boys look at each other furtively.

The mistress writes:

Maurice and Mickil stand up.

The mistress turns from the board.   The two boys stand.

MISTRESS. And what kept you so late?

Now, from the angle of the mistress, we see the benches, the seated children, and Maurice and Mickil standing. Mickil is pouting, getting ready to cry; he makes a little, whimpering noise.

MISTRESS'S VOICE. Have done with your snivelling and answer my question.

MAURICE. We weren't here in any place but when we were coming to school we met some kinsfolk of mine and they kept us talking.

MISTRESS. Isn't it a fine excuse you make up!   Go out now and cut a good fat rod and bring it in to me, my good boy, the way I won't hear any more of your blather.

Maurice goes out of the classroom.

We see him now walking across to a hedge outside the school, opening his penknife.

He seizes a stout branch, looks at it, lets it spring back.   He seizes another.   Still too stout.   He cuts off a thin branch, canes his own hand lightly, gently with it.

CUT to the same cane coming down hard on his outstretched hand.

TRACKBACK to see Maurice and Mickil before the mistress's table.

It is now Mickil's turn.   Three blows.   Maurice has his hands behind his back.

The mistress scolds them to the two posts at the end of the classroom

148

and ties them up and goes back to her blackboard. She wipes out the words about Maurice and Mickil and continues to chalk up the lesson.

DISSOLVE

Now the blackboard is entirely covered with the words and figures of the lesson.
Maurice and Mickil are still tied to the posts.
There is a knock at the door. The mistress turns around quickly, looks at the door and then looks at the two boys.
Another, sharper knock.
She hurries to the door and opens it.
The parish priest comes in.

CUT to

CLOSE SHOT of the two boys, who whisper delightedly to each other.

MAURICE. It is with us now, my boy.
MICKIL. You will see some sport.
MAURICE. It is now we have the bright smiles.

From the end of the classroom near the posts we see the priest talking to the mistress.

MICKIL. The devil take you, do you see the look on the mistress?
. . .

The priest, at the top of the classroom, is looking around him.

PRIEST. I see all of the children but Maurice and Mickil now . . . where are they in the world?
MAURICE ⎱ Here we are, Father.
MICKIL ⎰

The priest comes over from the top of the classroom towards us and towards the two boys.

PRIEST. Oh, what is the meaning of this? Who tied you here?
MAURICE. The mistress, Father.
PRIEST. And why?
MAURICE. I will tell you, Father. When Mickil and I were com⁄ing to school we met some kinsfolk of mine and they kept us talk⁄ing, the way we were an hour late.

As the priest beckons the mistress over, Maurice winks at Mickil.

PRIEST. What is this you are after doing to the poor little children?
MISTRESS. Oh, Father, I beg your pardon, I was for putting a little fear into them. . . .

Maurice shows his hands to the Father.

MAURICE. Look, Father . . .
PRIEST. Oh, my shame.

He turns to the mistress.

PRIEST. I will make short delay of putting you out of the school if you go on with this work. Untie them at once, and if I find that you set hands on them again you will have news to tell. . . .

After the first few words (and as the mistress unties the boys) the priest's speech is softened into the background so that we hear:

THE VOICE (softly). This was the first time I ever saw anger on a priest, and I said to myself that it comes on them as any other man . . .

CUT to

LONG SHOT of Maurice and Mickil running up the Hill of the Cairn, past the black bog, into the dusk. And as they run, call⁄ing to each other in the still evening, we hear:

THE VOICE. And the end of it was we had the rest of the day off, and we played, I remember, on the Hill of the Cairn till the dark came . . .

We follow the boys up the hill, and as the dusk grows deeper we hear:

THE VOICE. Was it that night, I wonder, that I dreamed a dream I have never forgotten? That night or another, who cares, for the tale of a man's life is beyond the bother of the clock and he must try to remember it the best he may . . .

And Maurice and Mickil have vanished into the darkness, and now there is nothing but darkness, and now again the darkness lifts and we are in a cottage room lit only by firelight. We move down the room, past dresser and table and chairs, and come to a bed where Maurice and Mickil lie together awake but silent. The Voice is talking throughout.

THE VOICE. I only know it was a winter's night, very wild, with the patter of snow on the window panes, and myself stretched out on the flat of my back in the fine cosy bed, and ever thinking of the Blasket.

We come closer and closer to Maurice and Mickil, and their eyes close and they fall asleep, the firelight moving their faces.

THE VOICE. But falling asleep, I was dreaming all of a sudden not of the Blasket at all but that Mickil Dick and I were walking through a fine green meadow, gathering flowers. When we had gathered our fill of them, we sat down, talking of school and brilla-bralla, as is the habit of children.

After a while it seemed that Mickil fell asleep—and I asleep that was dreaming it all. While I sat thinking what a strange thing was that same sleep, what would I see come out of his mouth but a pretty butterfly.

Through this we see a *LONG SHOT* of Maurice and Mickil walk-ing in a meadow, picking flowers. Half of the great meadow is in sunlight, half in deep dusk through which we see the strange shapes of trees moving and strange hills.

Closer now, we see the children sit down by a stream, their arms full of flowers. They sit in the sunlight. We hear birds singing above them, but, from a distance, we hear, too, the note of the owl as though it came from the dark half of the great meadow.

And closer still we see a butterfly above Mickil sleeping.

We see the butterfly fly away down the meadow.

Still it is flying.

Maurice is running along the sunlit meadow.

Still the butterfly is flying.

Maurice is running along the sunlit meadow towards the dusk. And as he runs, so the sunlight behind him grows suddenly dusky and the dusk before him lightens.

Still the butterfly is flying.

It flies on to a gate.

Birds are singing.

Beyond the gate with the butterfly perched upon it is a sunlit meadow.

Maurice is running towards the gate and the butterfly. And behind him is deep dusk, and the note of the owl.

He reaches the gate and the butterfly flies away, into the sunlit meadow.

And Maurice climbs the gate. And climbing the gate, he is suddenly in deep shadow.

With a spring he is over. Over into the sunlight.

Still the butterfly is flying.

In the meadow lies a horse's skull.

Maurice kneels by the skull.

The butterfly flies through the eyes of the skull.

The sunlit field is darkening, dusking.

The butterfly flies out of the mouth of the skull.

The butterfly is flying.

Maurice rises and runs through dusk towards the gate which stands at the entrance to a sunlit meadow.

The butterfly is flying.

Maurice climbs the gate, in deep shadow.

With a spring, he is in sunlight.

He runs along the sunlit meadow.

Mickil is lying asleep. The butterfly flies over his face, and is gone.

Maurice sits by his side, looking into Mickil's face.

Mickil wakes, yawns, stretches.

And we hear the voice of Maurice the child saying, as he sits by waking Mickil in the sunny meadow, by the stream:

MAURICE. It seems, when a man dreams, a white butterfly do be coming out of his mouth . . .

The meadow is sunlit no longer, but in deep dusk.   The deep dusk deepens into darkness.

Then it is light again, morning light, and we are in the cottage room again, by the bedside of the two boys.   Mickil is awake, sitting up, looking at Maurice, who is still speaking:

MAURICE. . . . and walking away; and when it comes again it is then he wakes.

And Mickil burst into a shout of laughter.   And Maurice awakes.

MICKIL. Och, listen to the way he is talking in his sleep . . .

And he bursts into laughter again . . .

CLOSE-UP of the two boys.

DISSOLVE

To CLOSE-UP of the two boys in the classroom, sitting on the bench . . .

We hear in the background a boy reciting his lesson.

MICKIL (whispering). And a butterfly was after coming out of my mouth.   Faith, it was my tongue!—like this . . .

Mickil puts out his tongue.

MAURICE. Put in your tongue or the pooka will bite it off.

MICKIL. It is all tales and hobgoblins with you, my boy . . .

The sound of the boy reciting in the background stops.

MAURICE. I had another dream.   I dreamed there were fine ships puffing up Dingle Market . . .

The mistress's voice cuts across Maurice's whisper.

MISTRESS'S VOICE. Maurice!
MICKIL (in a whisper). It is all over with us now. We are dead men.
MISTRESS'S VOICE. Come here.

Now we see Maurice go up to the mistress's table. He is holding out
his right hand, gingerly, in front of him, prepared for the worst.
A ragged boy, twisting his cap in his hands, stands by the table.

MISTRESS (sourly). It is you are the fine gentleman now. A mes-
sage has come that there is someone outside to speak to you . . .
MAURICE. It is my father, by God.

And Maurice runs out of the classroom.

CUT

At the entrance to the school stand Maurice's two aunts, his uncle
and another man with a parcel under his arm.
Maurice runs out excitedly, but stops when he sees them all and will
come no closer.
The mistress has followed Maurice and is standing on the threshold.
He stares at his uncle, then at the other man.

MAURICE. Is this my father?
FIRST AUNT. This is your father, Maurice.

And Maurice walks slowly up to his father, and his father embraces
him.

FATHER. Would you like to go home with me today?
MAURICE. I would indeed, what sort of place is it?
FATHER. Oh, a fine place.
MAURICE. Will we be going now?
FATHER. As soon as you have dressed in this nice suit of clothes
here, we will be going in the name of God.
MAURICE. Will there be trousers?
FATHER. Trousers, indeed, and a jacket, and a shirt, and a collar and
a cap and . . .

MAURICE. We will be going, surely. .... I will go in now so, and say goodbye to Mickil.

He walks into the school: quietly, a little stiffly and self-consciously: a small dignified boy in a child's smock.

In the classroom he stretches out his hand to Mickil. They stand for a few seconds, without speaking. We see them close. Then:

MAURICE (in a formal way, as befits a small boy about to become a man, but gently still, and with affection). Goodbye, Mickil, I am going home to the Blasket today and I hope I shall see you again in health and happiness.

But Mickil is still a child, and his eyes are full of tears.

MICKIL. Oh, so do I, so do I, Maurice . . .

CUT BACK to the entrance to the school. The mistress, on the top step, is talking down to the father.

MISTRESS. Indeed you should know what you are doing, taking the child home when he is just learning his scholarship, and if you left him here he would have a livelihood for ever . . .

FATHER. Och, my pity on your head, he's a boy from the Blasket Isles.

MISTRESS. And so he will lose his English and so he will be a fool when he grows up. Where and how will he get a job without the English?

FATHER. Isn't it better still for him to have the two languages? And another thing, you don't know yet what way Ireland will turn out. Faith, a boy should grow up at home, and his home is in the Isles.

MISTRESS (suddenly softens). The poor little child . . .

DISSOLVE

The road outside the school. The aunts and the uncle and the mistress are standing by a horse and cart. Along up the street towards them comes Maurice in his new breeches, jacket, shirt, collar, cap, shoes and black stockings, whistling a tune and taking steps as long as his father's.

The aunts and uncle greet him with delight, the women fussing around him.

FIRST AUNT. Faith, you are a grown man, God bless you.

SECOND AUNT. Turn round till I see the back now.

UNCLE. (Admiration in Irish.)

FIRST AUNT. They fit you as well as if the tailor had made them.

MAURICE. Oh, Father, I am a great sport for fineness.

And the two aunts kiss and fondle him, with little inarticulate murmurs, and make him show off his fine suit again and press money into his hand. And as he sulkily takes their kisses, in the embarrassed dignity of his new manhood, we hear:

THE VOICE (softly). Oh, don't I remember it now. I thought they were after tearing me asunder with their kisses, for women are the very devil for cuddling and coddling and all the like. Why wouldn't they take it fine and soft like a man?

The mistress, unsmiling, suddenly thrusts a coin in Maurice's hand. Then the father climbs into the cart, and the uncle after him, and Maurice after him. The aunts cling on to the sides of the cart. And now we see that the heads of the children of the school are peering round the door, Mickil's among them.

Maurice waves to the children on the steps, waves to his aunts.

And the cart starts off, rattling over the cobbles.

As it goes off we see the mistress hurrying towards the school, shooing the children with her hands.

The heads disappear.

Now we see, in *LONG SHOT*, the cart trotting along towards Slea Head.

Now, in *LONG SHOT*, it is moving towards the cliff head.

Now, close, it is stopping right on the wild cliff head in the noise of wind and sea, and Maurice is standing up in the cart staring down on the white crests of the sea.

MAURICE. Where? Where?

And the father points to the north-west, to the Blasket Islands.

THE FATHER. There to the north-west.   Over there.

And, from the cart stopped at the high, windy edge, we see the
island, and hear:

THE VOICE. I could not speak, a lump came in my throat.   I saw
little white houses huddled together in the middle of the island, a
great wild hill straight to the west with no more houses to be seen,
only a tower on the peak of the hill and the hillside white with
sheep.   I did not like the look of it.

MAURICE. But how will the horse and cart get over there?

THE FATHER. We will go in a curragh.

They all climb down from the cart.
A little way away from them.

MAURICE. But what sort of thing is a curragh?

They stand now on the cliff edge, looking out to the island: Maurice
small and still between the two tall men.

And suddenly the head of a man appears over the cliff edge, then his
shoulders, then his body, then he is all there, standing on the very
edge, the wind blowing his hair and his clothes.   There is no sign
of a path for him to have climbed.   He appears just like that: a
man, suddenly comes up over the cliff.

MAURICE. Oh, look, look, the man has come up out of the sea.

The man walks towards them.   There is a postbag on his back.

MAURICE. Oh, who is that, Father?   Did he fly up like a bird?

THE FATHER. Faith, he is the King of the Island . . .

MAURICE (in wonder). Do all kings come up like that?

And the King—a 'fine, courteous, mannerly, well-favoured man'—
approaches the two men and the boy.   And he greets the boy
first.

THE KING (in Irish). Musha, how are you now?

MAURICE (in English). Thank you very much.

THE KING. The devil, I think you have no understanding of the Irish . . .

MAURICE. I have not.

THE KING. You will.   And how does it please you to be going to the island?

MAURICE. It does not look too nice altogether . . .

THE KING. It does not neither, just a rock torn off the land and sitting down in the sea.   But there is no place like it in the world. Come down now.

And the King takes Maurice's hand and they walk to the very place on the edge of the cliff where the King had appeared, and the uncle waves his hand and gets into the cart and drives off, and the father follows Maurice and the King.

Maurice and the King stand on the cliff edge, the wind tumbling their hair and gusting about them.

Maurice looks down at the sea.

MAURICE. Do we jump?

But the King walks over the cliff, Maurice clutching his hand.   And they disappear.

From the cliff edge we look down at the King, Maurice and the father walking down a steep path to the quay and the many curraghs that are laid there.

And close we see Maurice pointing to the curraghs, and we hear:

THE VOICE (softly). Oh, do not I remember it now.   There on the quay were twenty black beetles twice as big as a cow . . .

And we hear Maurice's voice, following quickly on these words.

MAURICE. Do the big beetles bite?

And the two men and the boy walk on down again the steep path, and the King is shouting with laughter.   And an echo takes up his laughter.

And as the laughter echoes on, we PAN UP the high cliff.   Near the top of the cliff perches a big black bird.   And as the echo dies, we hear through the crashing of the sea waves:

MAURICE'S VOICE. Look at the big bird!   Oh, Lord, how do you keep your senses up there at all!

Now the father, the King and Maurice are walking along the quay, the sea noise greater.   And we see a curragh being carried from the slip, but we cannot see the man who carries it and it looks, indeed, as though the curragh is walking by itself.

MAURICE. Oh, the beetle!
THE FATHER. Faith, that's a curragh.
MAURICE. Do we go in that strange thing to the island?
THE FATHER. We do.

And Maurice is shaking his head, as one who would say: 'Lord help us.'

And now the curragh is afloat, and the King, the father and a fisherman are in it.   From the quay we see the curragh mounting the waves and hear:

THE VOICE. And in the black beetle with my father and the King we journeyed to the island.   This was the beginning and Dingle and the school had vanished entirely.

Now in *LONG SHOT*, the curragh is in mid bay, and we hear all the time the voice speaking:

THE VOICE. The wind had dropped.   There was not a breath in the sky, a dead calm now on the water, a wisp of smoke rising up straight from every chimney on the island, the sun as yellow as gold shining over the Pass of the Hill slopes from the west.   The beauty of the place filled my heart with delight.

And now, from the island, we see the curragh come in, and hear the voices of people and the barking of dogs; all echoing.
The curragh draws alongside the slip.   Maurice, the King and the father get out.   And from behind them on the slip we see people coming down by every path and children running, and dogs bark-

ing about their feet, all coming down towards Maurice.   And we hear:

The Voice. Oh, the island that day said Welcome, and Welcome.

And behind the voice we hear, softly, the echoing sound of Wel-come, Welcome, in Irish, called by many voices.
The crowd closes round the King, the father and Maurice, but it is the children who come most close to Maurice and they stare at him without speaking.
Now an old man, the grandfather, comes out of the crowd and walks towards Maurice, and the close circle of children is broken, and the grandfather embraces Maurice.

The Grandfather. Musha, God bless your life, my heart and my blood.
Maurice. Who are you?
The Grandfather. Och, isn't it a strange thing that you would not know your own grandfather.   You shall call me Daddo. Come up with me now . . .

The grandfather takes Maurice by the hand and together they climb up the path from the quay.   The children follow them, dancing and calling.   From the top of the path we see them climbing to-wards us. First one woman, then another, darts out of the crowd and kisses him, and we hear:

The Voice. Oh, the kisses they gave me then, the women of the island, I might have been a soldier returning from the holy wars but I would rather the frost than that to be done to me.

Now the grandfather and Maurice are walking past the village houses: long, low, narrow houses, many of them dug into the steep slope of the hill for shelter from the wind.   And old women hurry out of the houses and take Maurice in their arms and they mur-mur:

One Old Woman. Maurisheen, asthore.
Another Old Woman. Oh, my joy.
Another Old Woman. Welcome as summer coming . . .

And they all kiss him, and behind him are always the island children, staring at a wonder.

And as the last woman kisses him, we hear:

THE VOICE. A nasty habit in women, I thought, but I held my tongue.

Now the grandfather and Maurice come to the O'Sullivans' house. Two boys and two girls come out and stand, silent, at the door. The grandfather stops.

THE GRANDFATHER. Eileen, Maura, Shaun, Pierce . . .

And the four children step towards Maurice.

THE GRANDFATHER. Here is your brother, Maurice . . .

And the children move nearer Maurice, smiling; Brigid's arms are held open.

DISSOLVE

To the interior of the O'Sullivans' house, evening. The walls are bright with lime, a fine flowing fire sending warmth into every corner, a dog lying in the cinders, sugan chairs pushed back against the walls.   There is a spinning-wheel in a corner.

A young man is squatting near the hearth, playing a melodeon . . .

Boys and girls are dancing; Maura the sister is dancing alone among them.

The father and the grandfather sit at a table at the end of the room; there is a bottle on the table; all around them is the smoke of their pipes, and we see them through smoke; cloudy, immemorial peasant figures.

And the dancing goes on.

Then the boys and girls sit down on the floor, and clap their hands.

And shyly the sister Eileen steps out of the smoky darkness near the end table, and sings.

At the end of a verse, we hear, from the cloudy table, the voice of the grandfather crying:

GRANDFATHER. My love for ever, Eileen.

And as she sings, so children dance, we move again, and we move
slowly, around the room, to sad-and-gay music, round the firelit
hearth, the player, and the corner seat where Maurice, alone, half
dreaming, half awake, watches and listens, and the table of smokers
and drinkers, and Eileen's voice fades.

And then, out of that smoky end of the room, comes the voice of the
grandfather singing 'Eamonn Magaine'.

And moving away again, towards Maurice in his corner, we hear:

THE VOICE. I would feel a shiver of delight in my blood as I sat
listening that first evening of my homecoming, and it was no wonder, with the sweetness of the song and the tremor of the voices. I
did not understand the meaning of the words, but the voice and
the tremor and the sweetness were clear to me.

Very slowly the room is growing darker, but the music goes on.
And Maurice's head is nodding.

THE VOICE. . . . no wonder with the sweetness and the singing and
the noise of the sea and the darkness and the sweetness and the singing and the darkness . . .

And the voice fades slowly on the last words, and Maurice is asleep
in his chair in the darkening corner, and with the singing and the
music of the melodeon mingles the surging of the sea.

And, as the picture *FADES OUT*, we hear only the surging of the
sea.

FADE IN

To the sea breaking on the island cliffs.
Now a seagull is flying over the sea.
We follow the flight of a seagull over the sea towards the island.
We follow the flight of a seagull through the sky above the island.
We *PAN DOWN* the sky, from the flying seagull, to see, in
LONG SHOT, a man, a boy and an ass moving away towards
Hill Head . . .
Closer now we see that the man and the boy are the grandfather and
Maurice. And we hear Maurice's voice, and the grandfather's

162

voice closely, clearly, as though they were near us, though they are still in *LONG SHOT*.

MAURICE. Oh, it is a grand day to be on the island, Daddo.

THE GRANDFATHER. There is no place like it . . .

And now the *CAMERA* moves around the island. We see the Great Skellig and Skellig Michael, and Iveragh to the south-east, and herring-gulls around the trawlers in the bay. And over the sea sounds we hear the singing of larks.

MAURICE. Shall I be living here always and always, going after a load of turf with the old ass in the morning, or up at the sparrow's chirp to go lobster fishing with my father, or gathering the birds' eggs, or dragging the sea for herrings, or after the seals and the rabbits . . .?

THE GRANDFATHER. Och, the day will come . . .

And as the grandfather speaks, we *CUT* to him and Maurice, close, standing on Hill Head.

MAURICE. What day, Daddo?

We see them now from a low level so that they are great simple figures against the moving clouds.

THE GRANDFATHER. Let it be gone from your head now. It's a fine, grand day today, praise to God on high!

> There was music of birds flying over
> the green grass
> and little fish in hundreds
> frolicking in the nets . . .

MAURICE. Is that from a song?

THE GRANDFATHER. It is indeed, from an old song. Come now, boy. . . . Come.

He turns away . . .

CUT to the grandfather and Maurice loading turf on to the ass.

MAURICE. Were you ever away from the Blasket, Daddo?

THE GRANDFATHER. My sorrow, I spent a great part of my life going out to the islands all around, and it is little shoe or stocking was worn in those days, not even a drop of tea to be had, nor any thought of it.

MAURICE. No tea at all!

GRANDFATHER. There was no flour to be bought, no tea or sugar. Upon my word, it wasn't bad for that time. We had our food and our own clothes—the gathering of the strand, the hunt of the hill, the fish of the sea and the wool of the sheep. The devil a bit was there to buy some tobacco, and you could get a bundle of that for threepence. . . .

Many was the day we would leave the house at sunrise and we would not come home again until the blackness and the blindness of the night, myself and Stephen O'Donlevy . . .

And Pad Mor and Shaun O'Carna, dear God bless their souls, for they are all on the way of truth of now. . . .

Close, we see him straighten up from the loading of the turf, and look out at the sea. There are tears in his eyes.

THE GRANDFATHER. Did ye never hear how the life of man is divided? Twenty years a-growing, twenty years in blossom, twenty years a-stooping, and twenty years declining.

MAURICE. I never heard that before.

The grandfather smiles.

THE GRANDFATHER. Indeed, it is many things you have never heard before. Go on with you now. . . . Be happy when you can . . .

And now we see, in LONG SHOT, the grandfather, Maurice and the ass on the path towards the village. Maurice is running, scampering and dancing on all sides of the slow patiently moving old man and loaded ass.

Now Maurice is running along the strand of white sand towards the harbour. We hear, loud, the noise of the waves; and the barking of dogs we do not see, hollow, as though in caves; and the cries of the gulls.

Now with another boy, Tomas Owen Vaun, he is striding along the hill path towards Horse Sound, two dogs with them. The dogs run off into the deep grass and ferns and begin to bark: the high eager bark of the hunter. The boys run after them.

Now Maurice and Tomas are striding on towards the Scornach; they both have rabbits slung over their backs. And we hear:

THE VOICE. In a man's life there are twenty years a-growing. And here on the island, for me, they were growing slow to the din of the sea and the singing of ten thousand birds as I was up in the morning with Tomas and the dogs hunting the rabbits in the ferns after the shippens, the fat little puffins, and the seagulls' eggs on Scornach cliffs.

And, while the Voice speaks, we see Maurice and Tomas reaching the top of the Scornach. We look down, from their eyes, at the great cliff sickening to the sea. They put their rabbits in a hole, and Tomas begins to climb down the cliff, light as a goat through the screes. Maurice climbs, slowly and fearfully, after him: a long way after him.

And we look down from the clifftop and see Tomas far below us, and Maurice clinging on not so far below, staring up at us, the blue sea below him and all around him the great noise of birds. We hear, through wind, sea and birdery, the blown voice of Maurice crying.

MAURICE. Oh, holy Father, isn't it a dangerous place I am in?

He moves cautiously, along a cliff ridge. Great numbers of birds fly all around him.

Now, from below, we look up at the little figure of Maurice on the cliff face, and hear:

THE VOICE. Oh, kittiwakes, herring-gulls, puffins, guillemots, searavens, razorbills, black-backed gulls and petrels, you frighten the life out of a sinner with your crying and flying. . . .

And now, closer to Maurice, we see him groping in a burrow between the rocks, groping and digging and scratching. Suddenly he pulls out his hand. There is a baby puffin in it. And, holding the puffin out, he turns, perilously, and calls down the cliff:

MAURICE. Tomas ...

And the echo answers:

ECHO. Tomas.

And another echo, and another, and another; each farther off.
He moves about the face of the cliff, thrusting his hand into the hidden nests of the puffins.
Now on the cliff edge, we see Maurice climbing up, and over his shoulder is hanging a rope on which many puffins are tied together.
He reaches the clifftop, and flops down there, his puffins at his side.
Then he whistles down the cliff. And the echoes take the whistle and multiply it and throw it about in the wind and lose it.
And, after the echoes, comes:

TOMAS'S VOICE. I'm coming. ...

And soon he has climbed up to the clifftop, dirty and smiling. He has made a sack of his jersey, and hung it, heavy, over his back.

MAURICE. What have you got?
TOMAS. I have guillemots' eggs, razorbills' eggs and seagulls' eggs, my boy ... why didn't you come down with me?
MAURICE (slyly). Och, I was frightened. I got nothing at all.

And he rises and lifts up his bundle.

TOMAS. What have you there?
MAURICE (in a casual voice). Oh, puffins. Just puffins. Just thirty-six puffins, that's all. ...

And his casualness drops away from him, and he begins to dance, whirling his rope of birds. Now we see only the roped birds whirling.
Now we see only a skein of birds whirling through the sky.

TOMAS. Upon my word, you're a great hunter.

166

CUT BACK to Maurice.

MAURICE. I'm the happiest hunter on the hills of Kerry.

Now his birds are still.

TOMAS. Come to see if my eggs are clean now. . . .

And he moves away, Maurice following him after he takes up the
rabbits from the hole where they were left.

MAURICE. Can't you see they're clean, you little blind man.

Tomas stops at a big pool in a bog hole.

TOMAS. Look now, if this egg is hatching it will float on the water,
but if it is clean it will sink.

He throws in an egg.

CUT to the pool, the egg floating on it.

TOMAS'S VOICE. Och, the devil take it, there is a chick in that one.

Another egg lands on the water, and floats.

TOMAS'S VOICE. It is a good beginning.

Another egg lands, and floats.   And another, and another.
Now the surface of the pool is covered with red-and-black-spotted
eggs floating.

TOMAS'S VOICE. The devil a clean one among them.

Now Maurice takes his rope of puffins and cuts it in half, and hands
over half the puffins.

MAURICE. Look at us now!   Half apiece . . .

Tomas begins to laugh as he takes his share.

TOMAS. Look at us now, indeed.
MAURICE. I don't know why in the world you are laughing at me . . .
TOMAS. Because anybody would think you were an ape, you are so
dirty . . .

167

MAURICE. Faith, if I am dirty as you are, the yellow devil is on me.

Tomas, still laughing, begins to strip off his clothes; and Maurice
likewise.
We see them dive, naked, in the pool.
Now they are lying, half dressed, on the grass.
Tomas takes out a pipe and tobacco, and lights the pipe and puffs it
and passes it, silent, over to Maurice.
And Maurice takes it and puffs it and hands it back.
He lies flat on his back staring up at the sky.
There is music through bird and wind and sea noise.
Looking up, from Maurice's eyes, at the sunset sky, we see gulls
lazily wheeling.
We hear Tomas's voice singing softly . . .
Now the sky becomes blurred, and blurred birds seem to lurch across
it.

MAURICE'S VOICE. I'm thinking the tobacco is strong, Tomas, or a
most queer storm is a coming up . . .

CUT to Maurice and Tomas, Maurice now smoking.   Slowly he
hands over the pipe to Tomas and rises to his feet.
Now the two boys are walking back towards the village, their dogs
quiet at their heels, through the sea sounding sunsetting evening.
Maurice is a little unsteady on his feet.
Now we see the reflection, in water, of the houses of the village,
trembling with little spots of light.
Now we see the village itself, Maurice and Tomas walking through
it.
It is night nearly.   Lamps are lit in every house.
An old man stands at his doorway.

TOMAS. Are you well tonight, Puncan?
OLD MAN. Oh, musha, I was never so bad as I am today.

The boys pass on, laughing.

TOMAS. Isn't he always bad?   Good night, Maurice.

(N.B. Insert two more greetings with two villagers whom we will be
   seeing later.)
Tomas goes in at a cottage door.

MAURICE. Good night, Tomas.

Maurice walks on, one dog at his heels, and reaches his cottage.
The grandfather stands outside.
And Maurice stands by him.   He looks up at the climbing moon.

MAURICE. What a night it is, Daddo . . .
THE GRANDFATHER. And a fine gold moon over Cnoc-a-comma.
   Come in now before the potatoes get cold.

And he goes in.
And the moon climbs.

FADE OUT

FADE IN

To the calm sea in the full light of morning.
Over the sea a bird is flying.
The bird is flying towards the island.
The bird is flying above the harbour.

PANNING DOWN, we see that the quayside is crowded with
   people and that more are flocking down towards it on every path
   from the village.
We see, from the quay, a curragh coming in.
Now down a path run Maurice and some boys, and we hear:

THE VOICE. It is the custom of the island for everyone to be on the
   quay when the King is coming with the postbag from Dunquin . .

Maurice joins the crowd.   He sees Tomas in a group of children.

MAURICE (calling). Tomas . . .

Tomas runs over to Maurice, and a little girl, Mauraid, with him.

THE VOICE (continuing, even through Maurice's cry). ... with news from the mainland and stories from the length and breadth of Ireland and the rumours that do go about of what is happening in the wide world beyond ...

Now the King is standing on the quay, people all around him, making a deal of noise, chattering, arguing, questioning.

Now we see him, as he talks, from where Maurice and Tomas stand, the little girl Mauraid shy by their side.

THE KING (loudly).   Any man who has any spirit, let him take a curragh south to Ventry next Sunday.   There is going to be a great race in it.

Shaun Fada speaks from the crowd.

SHAUN FADA. They won't go, no fear of it.   Don't you see them yourself as lazy as any cripple from here to Belfast?

A VOICE. Listen to Shaun Fada.   He's so lazy ...

Another young man, Padrig O'Dala, speaks from the crowd.

PADRIG O'DALA. Did you hear of any curragh to be going in for it?

THE KING. Indeed there are—a curragh from the Cooas, one from Ballymore and another from Leitriuch.

The people press round the King again, talking and quarrelling, and he is lost to sight.

Children run away, up the village paths, their voices high, we hear:

CHILDREN'S VOICES. Are you going to the races?   I am now. Are you going, Padrig?

Close, we see Maurice and Tomas and Mauraid.

TOMAS. There'll be racing and dancing and games, all day long, and oh, the crowds!

MAURICE. Let's go ...

TOMAS. Oh, the devil, let's go ...

They turn from the quay and begin to climb up towards the village. Mauraid runs by their side.

MAURAID. Will you be after taking me too?

TOMAS. A girl!

MAURICE. Stay at home with you, Mauraid. Let the men be. Girls with their kissing and silly ways . . .

And Maurice and Tomas run on up the path . . .

Now we see the boys and girls of the island all gathered in groups in the village, talking.

Hens cluck and peck in the dirt.

Maurice and Tomas approach the gathering from different ends of the village. They meet on the fringe of a group of boys.

MAURICE (excited). What does your father say?

TOMAS. Arra, man, all I got was a clout on the back which threw me out on my mouth.

MAURICE. It is the same with me. We'll creep out unknown. Be up with the chirp of the sparrow, so . . .

Tomas winks.

MAURICE. Let's be pretending we cannot go, and set up a wail.

They join the group of boys near them . . .

A BOY. Are you going to the races?

TOMAS. Not me. . . . I had a cuff on the head for the asking.

MAURICE. Oh, sorrow, nor me. I was kicked out of the house like a football. It's a cruel world. Are you going yourself?

ANOTHER BOY. I am, indeed.

TOMAS. Oh, the luck of you.

And Maurice and Tomas go off, conspirators . . .

DISSOLVE to

The interior of Maurice's cottage. Moonlight through the window. The cottage is still and silent save for the ticking of the clock.

We hear, very softly:

THE VOICE. Tick tock, tick tock . . . believe me, my two eyes never closed . . . tick tock, tick tock . . . all the night awake in the moon-light I was waiting counting the tick tock of the clock . . .

As the Voice speaks, we *TRACK UP* slowly to Maurice's bed at the far end of the room.

Now the light of dawn comes through the window.

THE VOICE. . . . waiting for the dawn and the crying of the cock from Padrig's yard. . . . Then—up at a spring!

We see Maurice jump out of bed and begin to dress. He washes himself in a bowl of water, and cuts a bite of bread, and as he quickly dresses and washes and eats we hear:

THE VOICE. . . . an egg would not be broken under my feet for the lightness of my tread for fear I might be heard on the floor . . .

Then, stealthily, he opens the door and looks out at the early morning sky and runs down the village as we hear:

THE VOICE. Oh, the morning then would have raised the dead from their graves—an edge of golden cloud over Mount Eagle from the sun that was climbing in the east, a calm on the sea, not a stain in the sky and the lark singing sweetly above my head . . .

And now, in the wonderful morning, Maurice and Tomas are running down the village path towards the quay.

A voice calls to them.

A VOICE. Goodbye! Goodbye!

They stop for a moment and turn to look up to the top of the path. Mauraid stands there, alone, waving.

They wave back, and run on down to the quay.

A curragh is afloat, three men in it, another man about to climb in.

TOMAS. Hurry, hurry. . . . There's Shaun Tigue and Shaun Tomas
. . .

They rush up to the curragh.

MAURICE. Shaun, will you take us?
SHAUN TIGUE. Where are ye going?
TOMAS. The races!
MAURICE. The races!

Shaun Tigue beckons them to jump in.

Now the curragh is moving through the water, away from the island.

Now, from the curragh, we look back at the quay which is dotted with figures, and at the paths down which other figures are moving. . . . Now, from the curragh, we look back at the island.

Other curraghs are moving off from the island.

Now the curragh is in mid bay, guillemots, razorbills and petrels on the water, the four men stripped to their shirts rowing hard. Maurice and Tomas sit huddled together.

TOMAS. I was never on the sea so early . . .

MAURICE. It's you're the old stay-a-bed, boy.   The sea's been up and about all night . . .

TOMAS. When I am a man, I shall always be riding on the sea.   As soon as the dawn I'll be rowing and riding . . .

SHAUN TOMAS. When you are a man, you'll be tired of the sea . . .

TOMAS. Not me!

MAURICE. Not me! . . .

Shaun Tigue, in the bows, points to a big, white-breasted bird floating down with the tide.

SHAUN TIGUE. Do you see the loon?

MAURICE. Wouldn't you think it was a young gannet now?

Shamus Kate, an old man rowing in the middle, speaks as he rows, without looking up.

SHAMUS KATE. That is a bird never stepped on dry land . . .

SHAUN TOMAS. And where do they lay then, Shamus Kate?

SHAMUS KATE. Out on the sea . . . out on the sea.

SHAUN TIGUE. And wouldn't you say that the sea would carry off the egg?

SHAMUS KATE. On my oath it does not, for she lays it between her two thighs and she keeps it there till the chick is hatched.

MAURICE. I believe you. . . . Oh, the strange things!

Now the curragh is nearing the great cliff of the mainland.   They all take off their shoes and draw their trousers above their knees, and leap out and draw the boat over the stones above high water.

And Maurice and Tomas scramble into their shoes again, and are off, off up the cliff.

They run up the cliff, and are gone . . .

Now they are walking towards the chapel in Bally⁄na⁄houn.

They stop at the entrance to the chapel, and stand with many people there, but on the edge of the crowd.

MAURICE. What is this place?

TOMAS. Bally⁄na⁄houn, and farther than this I've never been in all my life . . .

He stares in wonder at the chapel.

TOMAS. Oh, isn't it a big house!   How was it built at all?

The people begin to go into the chapel, and Maurice and Tomas follow.

Inside the chapel, we see them, close, sitting in the last pew.

We hear, as a background, the voice of the priest.

Tomas is staring around him.   Suddenly he sees that a man in the front of the chapel has turned his head and is looking at him.

TOMAS (in a whisper). Oh, I'll be killed, my father is over there and he is looking at me.

Maurice looks, and sees that another man has turned his head to⁄wards them.

MAURICE (in a whisper). My father, too.   And Pierce.   Oh, they will kill us . . .

And the two boys bow their heads.

The voice of the priest rises.

CUT to

The outside of the chapel.

Maurice and Tomas run out and away from the chapel.   And then the rest of the worshippers come out.   Maurice's father and

Tomas's father look around them, the boys are but gone. The fathers smile and walk off with the others.

The boys are climbing the Hill of Classach. We see them, in *LONG SHOT*, climbing quickly.

Now they are on top of the hill. And, close to them now, we look down with them at the parish of Ventry.

TOMAS (in astonishment). Oh, Maurice!

And we see south over Ventry parish, and Maurhan parish, and north to Kill parish, green, flowered fields on all sides, a lonely house here and there away at the foot of the mountain, Ventry harbour lying south-east, three or four sailing-boats at anchor and a few curraghs beetling across the water.

TOMAS. Isn't Ireland wide and spacious now?

MAURICE. Oh, she is bigger than all this. I remember Dingle where I was long ago.

TOMAS. Where is that?

MAURICE (pointing). To the south of Mount Eagle . . .

TOMAS. Lord, I always thought there was nothing in Ireland, only the Blasket, and Dunquin, and Iveragh. . . . Oh, Maurice, it is a *grand* day we will have . . .

And at those words Tomas runs, goat-leaping, down the hill, towards Ventry parish, and Maurice runs after him.

They are walking through Ventry village. Many people are abroad, in their holiday best. Tomas eyes them with admiration.

MAURICE. Och, fine as paycocks, look at them strutting. The dandy men.

TOMAS. They must be millionaires, surely.

And the two boys walk on up the street, gazing everywhere with pride and wonder, until they reach a shop. They stop and look into the window. Over their shoulders we see the goods in the window: boots, cloth, tobacco, caps, groceries, tarred rope, apples and sweets.

MAURICE. There's toffee apples . . .

TOMAS. . . . and hard gums, and gobstoppers, and rock . . .

MAURICE. Oh, if we had money now . . .

TOMAS. Don't mind that . . . isn't it our brothers and sisters will be giving us the pennies?

MAURICE. Maybe . . .

They turn from the window, and sit on the ledge, facing the village street.

TOMAS. And what's more, when my father is drunk, believe me, it is easy to get money out of him.

They sit for a moment in silence. Visitors to the races pass them up and down the street. A young man with big shiny boots, tightly fitting trousers, a hard hat, a buttonhole, and a girl on his arm, passes by.

TOMAS. Who would that gay one be, I wonder . . . ?

MAURICE. Maybe he is the mayor . . .

TOMAS. The devil, they are coming!

Along the street towards them come Maurice's father and his brother Shaun and his sister Maura and Tomas's father . . .

MAURICE (in a whisper). Let on we are perished with the hunger . . .

And the two boys bend their heads as the others reach them.

MAURA. Musha, look where the two changelings are . . .

SHAUN. And how did you come to be here now . . . ?

MAURICE'S FATHER. It's no good talking. They would do anything they liked . . .

He puts a ten-shilling note in Maurice's hand and a crown in Tomas's.

TOMAS'S FATHER. Don't you know that youth does be gay?

He puts a ten-shilling note in Tomas's hand and a crown in Maurice's.

MAURICE'S FATHER. Off with ye now and spend the day as ye please . . .

176

And, laughing and smiling, the fathers and sister and brothers go off up the street, and Maurice and Tomas rush into the shop . . .

CUT to

Ventry strand.

There is a great crowd on the strand, and a great noise of hucksters shouting their wares and fair-men shouting their games and people laughing and bargaining and children being children.

The two boys stand and watch the crowd in amazement. A hurdy-gurdy is playing.

MAURICE. Did you ever see such a crowd?

TOMAS. Oh, Lord, where will food be found for them all?

They walk along the strand, past a hoop-la stall; and a little hand-worked roundabout and a man with rings and a stick to throw them on; and a cripple with a banjo, singing 'Danny Boy' through the noise of the invisible hurdy-gurdy; and a loud solitary man performing card tricks to an audience of half a dozen small children and an ass: he is shouting, 'Hallo, hallo, hallo! Come on, ladies and gentlemen: someone for the lucky club! Hallo, hallo, hallo!' A little farther along the strand is gathered a big bulk of people. Their laughter reaches the boys, and they run towards the crowd, towards the roaring wall of backs, and squeeze in to the front.

With them we see, in a cleared space on the sands before the crowd, a barrel and a man tucked inside it.

People are throwing blocks of wood at the barrel, trying to hit him. But they all miss, and after every shot the man sticks his head up and puts out his tongue.

And the man with the wooden blocks, near the barrel, is shouting:

THE MAN. Hurray, hurray, here is Sammy-in-the-Barrel willing to keep his head for any man. Three chances for a penny. Come on! Come on, lads! Come on, kill him, boys!

And Sammy-in-the-Barrel puts out his head and roars.

And Maurice nudges Tomas, and Tomas nudges Maurice, and at

last Maurice goes timidly out from the front of the crowd and buys three blocks.

Now, from behind him, we see Maurice take a shot. An old man with flowers in his hat stands, encouraging, by his side.

OLD MAN. A great shot, my love . . .

The block hits the edge of the barrel. And before Sammy has had time to put out his head, Maurice aims again. And up Sammy bobs to take it straight on the nose. He lets out a great howl.

The old man dances with delight, crying: 'Musha, my love for your hand for ever.' And the crowd shout. And Sammy drags himself out of the barrel, howling and cursing.

And Tomas rushes from the crowd and grabs Maurice and they both run off down the strand, behind them the noise of the crowd's laughter and Sammy's howling and the old man calling and the music of the hurdy-gurdy and the hoarse shouts of the card-man and 'Danny Boy', fading.

The boys run on over the strand. Suddenly they see four curraghs drawn up in line in the bay, the men stripped and their oars stretched forward.

Now, from behind them, we see them face on, jumping in the air, till they are on the edge of the strand. The strand is thickly lined with people, clattering, clamouring, disputing, praising, disparaging, like a swarm of bees buzzing on a fine day of harvest.

Now we are close to Maurice and Tomas; they sit on their heels on the rock; across them, across their hair wild in the wind and their sparkling eyes and their whistling lips, we see the four curraghs and the crews, bare to the waists, tensed ready; and we hear, scattered among the voices of the crowd, coming out clear for a moment then drowned again, blown away by the wind or the sea-din, these separate voices:

VOICES. A barrel on Ballymore . . .
Cooas Cooas Cooas . . .
My love for Ballydavid . . .
Leitriuch, Leitriuch . . .

178

whiz by like lightning . . .
Och, the killing of the cattle on you . . .
you are standing on my daughter . . .
Cooas Cooas . . .
A gallon for every baby in Ballymore . . .
Ballydavid . . .

TOMAS. Oh, Lord, now which is which in the world? Who shall we shout for? . . .

A voice shouts loud behind them.

VOICE. Shout for Cooas . . .

And, back now from Maurice and Tomas, we see that the voice belongs to an old man standing on a rock just behind them. He is a fat, tipsy old man, a bottle jutting from his pocket, with his tall hat tied on to his head by string . . .
Maurice wriggles round on his heels to the old man. He shouts through the noise.

MAURICE. Which curragh is Cooas?
OLD MAN. Oh, the devil take you, it's that one there . . . and Tigue Dermod in the middle of it . . .

The old man waves wildly, and we see the first curragh with a man as tall as a giant in the middle . . .
And we *PAN* from the first curragh along the other three as the voice of the old man continues shouting through the shouts of the crowd.

THE OLD MAN'S VOICE. And that's Ballydavid. And that's Leitriuch. And that's Ballymore.

Now we see the four curraghs.
A gunshot.
The curraghs race through the water.
We hear:

THE OLD MAN'S VOICE. Boo, boo, boo!

179

And we cut to the old man to see him dancing drunkenly on his rock, trying to pull off his hat, but the strings will not allow it.

THE OLD MAN. Pull Tigue, Tigue, Tigue . . .

CUT to the Cooas curragh.   The noise of the crowd rises.

CUT to the four curraghs racing.

MAURICE'S AND TOMAS'S VOICES. Pull Tigue . . .

CUT to Maurice and Tomas, shouting, squatting on their heels, pulling at the wind as if they themselves were racing.

MAURICE AND TOMAS. Tigue, Tigue, Tigue . . .

CUT to the Cooas curragh.

THE OLD MAN'S VOICE. Remember your ancestors! COOAS, Cooas . . .

CUT to the old man staggering on his rock as he shouts and dances and thrusts black tobacco into his mouth and shouts through the tobacco with the juice running down his chin . . .
And the boys' voices take the cry of 'Cooas Cooas' as we *CUT* to The four curraghs, the Cooas curragh leading . . .

THE OLD MAN'S VOICE. Bravo, Tigue. Bravo, bravo . . .

CUT to the old man.   Waving and shouting and chewing he slips off the rock and is up to his knees in the water . . .

CUT to the Cooas curragh pulling farther and farther from the other three.

THE OLD MAN'S VOICE (above the noise of the crowd). My love, my love . . .

CUT to the old man wading deeper into the water.

THE OLD MAN. My love to you for ever, oh, flower of men . . .

180

CUT to Maurice and Tomas laughing and clapping . . .

CUT to the Cooas curragh sweeping forwards. Tigue's oars are lifted high to show they are the victors . . .

CUT to the old man, deep in the water crying.

THE OLD MAN. Oh, flower of men! Flower of men!

And at last, with a great heave, he tears his hat off his head and sends it skimming across the water.

Now Maurice and Tomas run, with the whole running crowd, towards the slip.

Now the crowds are at the slip, but they do not stop. They wade out into the sea to the curraghs, stretching out their hands. The old man is leading them.

From a curragh we see the crowd reach the Cooas crew near us, and the old man, hatless, tears pouring from his eyes, grasping the hands of Tigue Dermod and crying, up to his waist in water:

THE OLD MAN. Man beyond all men! Musha, love of my heart, my little jug . . .

And other hands are grasping Tigue and the rest of the crew.

Now from the slip we see the curragh, and all inside it, lifted high on a hundred hands and borne towards us.

And now the Cooas crew and the crowd throng from the slip up towards the village. We see them approaching us, the grand Tigue and the dripping-wet old man arm-in-arm at the head of the procession.

CUT to

Maurice and Tomas, arm-in-arm too, like two small victors, marching at the end of the procession.

The procession moves into the public house.

CUT to Maurice and Tomas entering the public house.

From the door we look into the packed bar. In the middle of the floor stands Tigue Dermod, a gallon pot in his hand. The old man is handing gallons over from the bar to the Cooas crew and their supporters laughing and crowding around them.

We move slowly into the bar, towards the counter and the backs of drinking men. We move up to the backs of a group of tall and burly men. And we see, between them, little Maurice and little Tomas.

Between the shoulders of the burly drinkers we see the face of the barmaid smiling down at the two boys, whose heads are only just above the counter.

Now, from behind the counter, we see the heads of the two boys, and hear:

MAURICE (in an unnaturally deep voice). Two pints.

The barmaid laughs.

THE BARMAID. Two pints? And have ye money?
MAURICE AND TOMAS. We have.

The barmaid pushes two pints across to them. Maurice pays.
From behind the counter still we see the faces of the two boys very close.

MAURICE (to Tomas, in a whisper). Maybe it will make us drunk.
TOMAS. Not us.
MAURICE. Did you ever drink before?
TOMAS. Arra, man, I did, that night they had the barrel in the house of Dermod O'Shea. I drank a pint and never got drunk.

We see Maurice's hand come up with the pint pot. Then his face is buried in it. We see only the heads of the two boys: Tomas looking at Maurice, and Maurice half hidden behind his pint. Then the pint is lowered.

MAURICE. It is good.

Up comes Tomas's pint. Maurice looks on with interest. Down comes the pint.

TOMAS. Oh, it has a foul taste, I will never drink it.

MAURICE. I will tell you why you get a foul taste in it. It is because you are only sipping it. When you raise your glass to your mouth, make no stop till you have to draw breath.

Both pint pots are now raised. We see only the two heads half hidden behind the pots, and the fingers clutching the handles. Down the pots come.

TOMAS. I think you are right. Let us have another.

His hand brings down his pot with two bangs on the counter.

Now, from behind the counter, across the full and empty pots and bottles, and through the crowd of drinkers against the bar, we see the Cooas crew in the middle of the floor, the old man among them. They all have gallon measures in their hands. They are all drunk. The old man stands on his toes and puts his hand on the muscles of Tigue's arm. Tigue is drinking. The great arm is raised to hold the gallon.

THE OLD MAN. Musha, musha, isn't strength a fine thing!

Tigue lowers his gallon, and opens his mighty mouth.

TIGUE (in a high, hoarse, weak voice). Up Cooas! Up Cooas!

And he drinks again.

THE OLD MAN. Up Cooas! Up Cooas!

Sea-water drips from his clothes.

A hand stretches out from the crowd near him and takes the old man by the hair.

THE OWNER OF THE HAND. What the devil is that talk. Bally-more. Ballymore.

Closer now, we see Tigue slowly lower his gallon and raise a great knotted fist.

TIGUE (to the owner of the hand, in his high weak voice). If I let down this sledgehammer you will be dead . . .

They all laugh . . .

The hand lets go of the old man's hair.

THE OLD MAN. Cooas, Cooas . . .

CUT to Maurice and Tomas, seen from behind the counter.

TOMAS. I will fight him myself . . .
MAURICE. I will hold your coat.

And suddenly the laughter of the bar is blurred. We hear, through
the blurred laughter and the thick cries:

THE VOICE. A man will always remember the unpleasant things
that do happen, and I remember that at that moment the house be-
gan to go round me like a laughing top. . . . There were two
Tomases where there was only one before, and he reeling like a man
in a high wind . . .

We see Tomas blurred and wavering, and hear Maurice's voice.

MAURICE (in a small voice). Something ails me, Tomas . . .

And the blurred laughter rises.
Now, from the street outside, we see Maurice and Tomas weaving
out of the pub.

MAURICE. Your face is green, Tomas Owen Vaun.
TOMAS. Arra, man, it is not, I could drink a barrel of it yet . . .

And with these words Tomas falls against a wall. And they both,
their backs to us, lean over the wall. And looking at the two
boys leaning over the wall, we hear:

THE VOICE. Isn't it great folly for any man to be drinking at all, I
thought. And isn't it youth that's foolish. And this is the last
time, indeed, I thought. And oh, dear, dear, dear . . .

DISSOLVE to

Maurice and Tomas walking on the road from the village of Ventry,
and away from us.
The sun is sinking.

Many people are taking the road also. They pass us, down the road, into the sunset. The cripple with his banjo under his arm; an old man pushing his hurdy-gurdy; children silently sucking sweets, half sleeping as they walk, clutching their mothers' or fathers' hands; Sammy-in-the-Barrel, with his barrel on his back; couples arm-in-arm; two drunk tinkers; a young man playing the melodeon as he goes.

DISSOLVE to

A curragh moving over the moonlit sea towards the island.
The music of the melodeon is heard in the distance, and the voices of men far off.
Closer now, we see that in the curragh are Maurice's father and brother and sister, and Tomas's father and brother, and Maurice and Tomas in the stern.
And Tomas's brother is singing 'Skellig's Boy', fine and slowly and softly.
We are close now to the stern.

MAURICE (softly, lazily half asleep). Oh, what a day! I never thought there was such a day to be had in all the world! Oh, the games and the singing and the shouting and the racing . . .

Tomas is eating a stick of rock.

TOMAS. I'm thinking that sweets are nicer than porter, Maurice . . .
MAURICE (very softly). Such a day . . .

Now in *LONG SHOT*, the curragh is moving through moonlight near to the island.
And from the distant, unseen mainland, we hear a crying and an echoing of:
> 'Cooas Cooas
> Ho-lee-ho-hup-
> Ho-lee-ho-hup',
a crying and an echoing, and then a fading of all sound.

FADE OUT

FADE IN

On the island village. Bright morning light. We move along the village, slowly. As we move, we hear:

THE VOICE. Every day was a fine, grand day, sun or rain, for a growing boy on the sweet wild island, I thought then and I think still. . . . Going to school in the mornings, I would wish my neighbours the good day as they were working or setting about their work or sitting in the sun . . .

We are moving along the village slowly: the village awake and at work.

At a cottage door sits, on a sugan chair, the Puncan of the village. His arms are folded, he is chewing tobacco.

MAURICE'S VOICE. Good morning to ye, Puncan.

The Puncan spits.

THE PUNCAN. Faith, I have seen better . . .

We move on.

Outside a cottage Shaun Teague and Shaun Tomas are setting out their nets in the sun.

MAURICE'S VOICE. Good morning, Shaun Teague and Shaun Tomas. How will be the mackerel tonight?

They go on setting the nets.

SHAUN TEAGUE. Och, there'll be plenty, with all the gannets about, there was never such a day for them . . .

We move on. Outside a cottage two women are washing clothes in a tub.

MAURICE'S VOICE. Good morning to ye, Kate O'Shea and Kate Joseph . . .

They go on washing.

KATE O'SHEA. Good morning to ye, Maurice. (To Kate Joseph)

186

Did you ever see such a shirt in all your life?... I'm thinking all the dogs in the island have been after chewing the tail...

We move on, the words trailing after us. Outside a cottage Padrig O'Dala and Tomas's father and Paddy Tim are mending their lobster pots...

MAURICE'S VOICE. Good morning to ye.
TOMAS'S FATHER. Tell Tomas not to be forgetting the turf after school now...

We move on. Outside a cottage, Mauraid is scattering food for the chickens which cluck and peck all around her...

MAURICE'S VOICE. Good morning, Mauraid...

She looks up and smiles.

MAURAID (shyly). Good morning to ye, Maurice.... Will you be on the cliff tonight to see the fishing?

We move on.

MAURICE. Arra, I will.
MAURAID. Shall I look at the fishing with you, Maurice?

We move on, her words trailing after us, on along the clustered village with its men working at pots and nets, sharpening tools, cutting wood, and a clatter of pots and pans and the sound of women's voices coming out of the open cottages...

THE VOICE. Or on days when there was no school, maybe I would be lying with my daddo, stretched out on the turf, gazing down at the fish-filled sea...

And as the voice speaks, the picture *DISSOLVES* to the cliffs, and we *PAN* along the cliffs to where the figures of Maurice and the grandfather are lying. Closer to them, we see that the grandfather's eyes are closed in sleep. Maurice is lying on his belly, looking out to sea. It is afternoon.

MAURICE. Do you know where I am looking, Daddo? I am look-

187

ing at America. Oh, it is a fine place surely, all its chimneys touching the sky and everybody rich as captains. .... Do you think that I will ever be going to America when I am a young man, Daddo?

The grandfather does not answer.

MAURICE. Daddo, Daddo ...

Maurice turns around and looks at the old man sleeping, and we hear:

THE VOICE. I remember thinking, looking down at the face of the old man asleep ...

MAURICE'S VOICE. You were one day in the flower of youth, but, my sorrow, the skin of your brow is wrinkled now and the hair on your head is grey. You are without suppleness in your limbs and without pleasure in the grand view to be seen from this hill. But, alas, if I live, some day I will be as you are now ...

As Maurice gazes at the old man asleep, and as we hear his voice, his lips do not move.

Now Maurice puts out his hand and gently pulls the old man's beard. The old man opens his eyes.

THE GRANDFATHER. Oh, Mirrisheen, I fell asleep. Am I long in it?
MAURICE. Not long at all.
THE GRANDFATHER. And were you speaking to me in my sleep? I seem to have heard your voice, a long way away ...
MAURICE. I was letting on I could see America across the water but all I could see were the waves and the old gulls. .... Shall I ever be going to America, Daddo?
THE GRANDFATHER. Upon my word, it is likely. The young are ever after going away over the water, and they leave the old country cold and poor as a house without children ...
MAURICE. Then I shall stay on the island then, and be a fine fisher⁄man ...
THE GRANDFATHER. Musha, my heart, a man of the sea never had a good life and never will ...

MAURICE. Och, where I shall go then?

THE GRANDFATHER. I don't know what way you will go but only to follow your nose in the end of all.

And as he speaks the grandfather is filling and lighting his pipe. And when it is alight Maurice takes out of his own pocket a blackened clay and lights it, bowl to bowl, from the grandfather's pipe. He draws the smoke down deep, and the old man smiles. They lie together, over the noisy sea, smoking and smiling . . .

DISSOLVE to

The sea. It is evening.

A bird is flying over the sea.

A bird is flying over many, many curraghs out on the sea.

A bird is flying over the cliffs of the island.

We *PAN DOWN* on to the cliffs above the strand.

All the women of the village are sitting on their haunches on the edge of the cliff, looking out at the curraghs.

Behind them along the cliff stand old men and children, Maurice and the grandfather and Tomas among them. And we hear:

THE VOICE. And on a night of mackerel fishing I would stand among the children and the old men of the village on the cliff over the strand, looking out at the curraghs and hearing the women calling and crying across the water to their men . . .

Close now to the women on their haunches, we hear:

ONE WOMAN. Your soul to the devil, throw the head of your net be-hind them . . .

She is waving her arms, her hair is streaming in the wind . . .

KATE O'SHEA (screaming). Tigue, Tigue, draw in your nets. . . . Och, my pity to be married to you, you good-for-nothing . . .

ANOTHER WOMAN. My love for ever, Dermod . . .

KATE O'SHEA. Pull to the south with you . . . aie, aie . . .

A voice comes back across the water from the curraghs.

A Voice. May the yellow devil fly away with you . . .

Another Woman. Over there! Over there! Patrick, are you stone blind . . .?

And all the women are calling and crying, Kate O'Shea screaming in Irish at the top of her lungs.   Their shawls are thrown off, they are flailing the wind with their arms.

Now close to a group of old men near the roaring women, we hear:

First Old Man (groaning). Ooooh . . .

Second Old Man. Arra, what ails thee?

First Old Man. What ails me is a pain in my head listening to those seal-cows of women . . .

Third Old Man (pointing to Kate O'Shea). Kate is giving out . . .

And Kate is now only croaking curses . . .

Second Old Man. The devil a wonder short of her having a throat of iron . . .

First Old Man. She can croak louder than a bull-seal can bellow. . . . Och, to be married to a thunderclap . . .

But all the noise of the women is suddenly hushed.

We are close now to Maurice and the grandfather.

The Grandfather. Look boy, your father is drawing in his net . . .

And now, on the water, we see Maurice's father in his curragh drawing up the heavy net, every mesh with a fish in it.

The air is loud with the roaring of the sea and the splashing and thrashing of the mackerel and the creak of the curraghs, and through all the noise we hear the voices from the clifftop, close at our ears:

First Old Man. Musha, it is straight down with fish . . .

Second Old Man. O Lord, O Lord, I doubt he won't land all he had . . .

Third Old Man. Look at him now, he is cutting the net . . .

And, from close on the water, we see Maurice's father cutting his nets.

FIRST OLD MAN. Och, the lucky man who gets the cut piece of the net, it is *all* his . . .

And now there is a commotion among the curraghs . . . They all begin rushing up to get the cut piece of the net.

SECOND OLD MAN. Lord, Lord, how many mackerel are there then in the sea?

THIRD OLD MAN. Praise to God for His gifts . . .

Now the cut piece of the net is drawn up into a curragh.

Now the curragh of Maurice's father is moving across the shining sea.

Now, from the water, close to the cliff, we look up at the women on the edge: a long line of women, squatting on their haunches, shawls over their heads, silent, utterly unmoving against the darkening sky.

And we hear, softly, a woman's voice, the voice of Kate O'Shea:

KATE O'SHEA. Praise to God for His gifts.

DISSOLVE to

The interior of Maurice's cottage.   Close, we see a table piled with apples and oranges and sweets and cakes and tarts, and we hear voices and the laughter of young girls, and the noise of the wind outside.

We *TRACK* back to see the whole room; the lamps alight, a great peat fire burning, the ticking clock.

Maurice's sisters, Maura and Eileen, are busy at the hearth and over the pots on the fire.   Mauraid is scattering white sand on the floor.   Other girls are washing plates and setting knives and forks on the table.   And we hear:

THE VOICE. Praise to God for His gifts,
for a roof and a fire,
a red red fire in the cold winter night

in a house on the edge of the seas.
And the wind be wild and the house do be bright . . .
and the girls do be as busy as bees . . .
Winter had come to the island, and Halloween was upon us, and outside in the blowing dark the boys were hunting thrushes.

And we are outside the house now, on the wild island: the island thrown up black against the phosphorous sea.
We see the bobbing pinpoints of lanterns on the stormy cliffs.
Now we are closer to the cliffs.   Three lanterns bob towards us, and then stop.   In their light we see the faces of Maurice and Tomas and a youth, Padrig Peg . . .
Padrig lifts his hand out of his oilskin pocket.
We see the hand close, in the lantern light.   It is full of dead thrushes.

PADRIG. Six.

Tomas puts out his hand.

TOMAS. Three here.

Maurice puts out his hand.

MAURICE. One.   I had my hands around two more but they pecked me like puffins.

A bird's cry—giog-giog-giog—comes out of the darkness.

MAURICE (whispering). What is that?
PADRIG. It is a peewit. . . . It's blinded in the light. . . . What did you think it was . . . ?

Padrig thrusts his hand into a sparse and wind-blown bush and pulls out the bird still crying.   The crying stops.

PADRIG. Now we will go down Seal Cove. . . . Quiet!   Dead quiet!   Take it fine and easy.   Don't be afraid.

CUT

Now we see, from the cliff edge, the three lanterns bobbing down the cliff. The noise of the sea shouts up to us. Blackness, and the three lights bobbing. Blackness, and the hollow shouting of the sea.

CUT

Now we are close to the three boys standing in the cove. They move their lanterns slowly in half-circles, illuminating the great rocks and the sea breaking upon them, and we hear:

THE VOICE (softly). You would think the living and the dead were there with the roar of the waves and the hiss of foam . . .

PADRIG. Don't be afraid. And don't speak a word till we get across to the patch of soil there. The thrushes are all sleeping now . . .

Now we see the lanterns bobbing across the cove, and across the crevice and the patch of soil.

Close, we see Padrig thrust his hand into the crevice and draw out a thrush. And again. And again. And again. As he is capturing the sleeping birds, so Maurice and Tomas, moving their lanterns to light the battering sea, speak fearfully:

TOMAS. Are you afraid at all?

MAURICE. The devil a bit . . .

TOMAS. It's often my father told me that people had been heard speaking here . . .

MAURICE. Oh, whisht, Tomas, do not say that. . . .

TOMAS. But they were not people indeed.

MAURICE. Faith, it is I know they were not. . . .

Now from another part of the cove we see the wavering lanterns, we see mighty waves roaring in and crashing on the rocks.

Now the three lanterns' lights move up the cliff.

Now from the edge of the cliff we look down on to the three lights climbing up towards us. They come closer. We see, in the lantern light, the three boys scrambling up and clinging on to one another's coat tails.

Now the light is blindingly near us.

And now we are back in the bright cottage, at the end of the room farthest from the door. It is full of boys and girls. The girls are beginning to pluck the sparrows heaped on a table.

The door is flung open. The wind hurling in, and then Maurice and Thomas and Padrig, spindrift-wet and wild-haired.

There is a noise in the house, of the voices of children merry together, and a boy calls out, and his cry is taken up by other voices, as the three enter.

A Boy. How many have you?
Another Boy. How many now . . .?
Another Boy. Oh, look at them all . . .
A Boy. I got twenty . . .
Padrig. Faith, we have twenty-eight . . .

The three throw their thrushes on to a table . . .

CUT to

The thrushes roasting on the fire. We hear the music of a melodeon.
PAN ALONG the room slowly from the fire.

A young man is sitting on the floor, back against the wall, playing the melodeon. . . .

Four girls and four boys are dancing a set, which is a dance like the old quadrille.

Boys and girls are sitting at the table, eating. Some stand, eating the little roasted birds with their fingers, watching the dancing.

A girl is sitting on a boy's knee.

Boys are leaping up at a big apple hung by a rope from the rafters, trying to take bites out of it.

Now we are close to a tub of water and a little group of boys and girls, Mauraid and Maurice among them, kneeling around it.

A boy and a girl, at the same time, throw a bean each into the water.

Mauraid (softly, looking at Maurice). If the beans sink in the water, it is a sign that Michael and Brigid do love one another. . . .
The Girl Brigid. Och, they are floating. . . .

194

Mauraid puts a bean in Maurice's hand.

MAURAID. Will you try?

Maurice throws the bean into the water, and, as he does so, Mauraid
    throws one in also.
We see the beans sink in the water. . . .
Now we see close the faces of Mauraid and Maurice.
And now nearly all the boys and girls are dancing.   The melodeon
    is playing a gay tune.   Maurice is dancing with Mauraid . . . the
    music rises.

FADE OUT

FADE IN

On the sea.
The sea is violent.
The sea is still.
The sea breaks against the rocks.
The sea laps the rocks.
A bird is flying over the rough sea.
A bird is flying over the calm sea.
A bird is flying over the sea.
A bird is flying over a single curragh on the sea.
And through this we hear:

THE VOICE. The life of a boy a-growing
    on the little island
    was a great coming and going;
    sea loud or silent
    as a flock of snowing—
    a great coming and going
    of the weathers and the birds
    and the seasons and the tides
    and the singing of the Irish words
    and the love of the world besides . . .

And behind the words of the Voice, and through the changing
voices of the wind and the sea, we hear the same words very
softly spoken in Irish.

And now we are close to the curragh, and Maurice and Padrig Peg
and the grandfather are sitting and rowing there.

THE VOICE. Fishing for mackerel or herring
in the Great Sound
or out after pollock on the Wild Bank
where the cries of a million birds were falling—
riding the wild waves in a Samhain wind
or turning in spring time
to the island of Inish Vickallaun—
There was so much to be done
under the moon and the sun
I cared for nothing
save the island people and the island ways
and the great passing of the days
to the sounding of the waves . . .

Through the words of the Voice we see the curragh in the Great
Sound, and on the Wild Bank; we see the nets raised, empty and
full; we see the curragh moving on choppy and on glassy water.

Now we are close to the curragh again, Maurice and Padrig and the
grandfather there with dogs at their feet.

THE GRANDFATHER. Do you see the house on the Inish now?

The grandfather points out to the Inish Island.

MAURICE. I do not.

THE GRANDFATHER. Look carefully at the middle of the island and
you will see the sun sparkling on something. . . .

From the curragh, we see the house high on the Inish, caught in the
sun.

PADRIG. It was there I was born, but only the birds and the beasts do
live there now.

THE GRANDFATHER. It was once a fine place; now the weeds grow over the paths and all the houses but the one are fallen in the wind and the rain.

Now the curragh is closer to the Inish.

MAURICE. Oh, listen, listen.

And we hear from the Inish a noise which takes an echo out of the coves. Gurla-gu-hu-hu-golagon! Gurla-gu-hu-hu-golagon!

THE GRANDFATHER (smiling). Have I not told you often that spirits are to be seen and fairy music to be heard above in the Inish?
MAURICE. What is it, Daddo?
THE GRANDFATHER. Row on, row on . . .

Again we hear the noise of Gurla-gu-hu-hu-golagon! And its echo the coves.
Now the curragh is closer to the Inish.

PADRIG. Look in now, and keep your eyes on the shingle . . .

And we see, from the water, a great number of seals stretched at full length, sunning themselves on the strand.

MAURICE'S VOICE. Och, the seals are sleeping in the sun . . .
THE GRANDFATHER'S VOICE. And do you think they are sleep-ing? Look, boy. . . .

We hear the grandfather and Padrig give a great roar.
The seals raise their heads.
Then away with them to the water, at a wonderful swiftness.
They are spouting in the water.
Now we are close to the strand; not a seal to be seen, save only the rings they have left in their wake.
Now Maurice, the grandfather and Padrig are climbing an old path up the Inish cliff.
Now they are within sight of the house at the foot of a little hill.
The dogs are barking and chasing in and out of the ferns, the tall grass and the bracken. We see rabbits running.

197

Now we are near the house: a little low hut with a felt roof, ruins in plenty around, weeds and nettles growing among them. The dogs, each with a rabbit in his mouth, run up to the two men and the boy, who take the rabbits away from them.

The men and the boy stand alone on the island in the setting sun.

THE GRANDFATHER. The house of Shaun O'Carna stood there.

We see a few pieces of rotten wood in the deep and tangled grass. And we *PAN* along the nettled and weedy wilderness. . . .

PADRIG'S VOICE. Here my father was born and his father before him —there was the schoolroom there—here were the fine paths where we climbed up to the sheep on the hills—there was singing and dancing and great story-telling in all the fine stone houses—nothing now, nothing, nothing . . .

CUT BACK to the three.

THE GRANDFATHER. My sorrow, the day will come when the Blasket is empty too and the houses in ruin and nothing to be seen but the green grass.

MAURICE. Faith, never, Daddo.

THE GRANDFATHER. The young will be going away from the island, as they went away from this place—over the sea to America, into the towns and the cities . . .

The sun is setting behind the Foze Rocks, and nothing to be seen beyond them but the sky like a great shining wall.

Now the three are moving up the little hill, the grandfather's voice continuing.

GRANDFATHER'S VOICE. . . . the young will go and the old will be left. And after the old are dead and are on the way to truth, there will be no more fishing nor hunting nor fowling on the island and all will be ruin . . .

We are in the churchyard half way through the grandfather's words, by the old chapel. The two men and the boy are standing in the middle of the churchyard. Above the ruin is a cross.

THE GRANDFATHER (softly). Maybe it will come that *all* the little islands, *all* the little places where men do make a livelihood together out of the gathering of the strand and the hunt of the hill and the fish of the sea will be empty and forgotten . . .

MAURICE. I shall stay on the island . . .

THE GRANDFATHER (smiling). You will be most lonely, for you will be the only one. . . . Come now, let us go down to the little house. . . .

And they move away out of the darkening churchyard.

DISSOLVE to

The entrance of the Inish house. The grandfather opens the door. Maurice peers past him into the room. We see the room from Maurice's angle. The walls are whitened with flaking lime. A rabbit scampers out of the room through a hole in the wall.

Now, from the end of the room opposite the door we see the grandfather enter, followed by Maurice and Padrig.

The grandfather crosses to the hearth, his arms full of ferns. He kneels and begins to make a fire of the ferns, saying over his shoulder:

THE GRANDFATHER. You be going out and laying traps for the morning, Padrig. Maurice, open two of the rabbits now and hang the other two outside the house. . . .

He lights the fern.

CUT to Padrig sweeping the floor of the room with a brush of ferns.

CUT to Maurice skinning the rabbits with his knife.

CUT to two rabbits hung on a nail outside the window in the deepening darkness.

CUT to the grandfather, Maurice and Padrig sitting, the old man in a broken chair, the others on fern heaps on the floor, near the fire, eating from a steaming pot.   A lantern is lit.   Moonlight streams through the window on to the fire and the seated figures.   We hear the noises of the wind and the sea.

They have finished eating.   The two men light their pipes.

MAURICE. I think I can hear the seals.   Olagon olagon.

And we hear, through wind and sea, the far noise of the seals.

MAURICE. I wonder, Daddo, would you believe that the seals are people put under magic?

He looks up at the old man, his face white in the moonlight.

PADRIG. I have heard it, and upon my word I would believe it, for they are just like old women keening.

THE GRANDFATHER. Some years ago there was a man went from the Blasket hunting the seals, about the month of November, because the young seals were born.   It was back in Bird Cove it happened. . . .

In moonlight and firelight Padrig and Maurice on the ferns stare up at the old man speaking, his pipe a-glowing.

THE GRANDFATHER. When he came out of the boat he saw a young seal up in the head of the cove.   He went up after it, stick in hand, as was the custom when they went seal-hunting. . . .

MAURICE (in a whisper). Yes, yes . . .

THE GRANDFATHER. And the cow-seal leapt straight at him, snarl-ing.   But he clambered up on the ledge on the side of the cove, and when he had reached it, would you believe it, the cow-seal spoke out to him.   'If you are in luck', said she, 'you will leave this cove in haste, for be it known to you that you will not easily kill my young son'; and she went back again to her young one. 'For the sake of the world,' the man cried out to his mate in the boat, 'back her in as quick as you can.'   And they were off.   And from that day till the day he died, that man never saw a day's health. . . .

MAURICE (softly). Faith, I believe it. . . .

Now in the moonlit room—the fire and lantern out—the two men and the boy lie, each in a corner, on a bed of ferns. . . .

Close to Maurice, we see that he is not sleeping but that his eyes are wide open. . . . He is looking up at the moonlit night through the cobwebbed window.

We look up at the night from Maurice's angle. The two rabbits hang on a nail outside, at the side of the window, moving slightly in the wind, half-dancing on air.

We see a hand, an arm, pass across the window to the rabbits. The hand lifts the rabbits off the nail.

Very close to Maurice, we see his eyes strained wide, his mouth rounded. We hear his terrified whisper: 'O Lord, save me from the fairies.'

As the hand, dangling the rabbits, slowly draws back across the window and vanishes, Maurice screams.

He leaps to his feet, runs over to Padrig, kicks him.

Padrig turns in bed.

PADRIG (sleepily). What ails you?

MAURICE. Oh, oh, Padrig, it is something I saw outside going off with the rabbits . . . a long hooking hand . . .

PADRIG. Musha, my pity for your brass head. Go to sleeeep . . .

He turns back to sleep.

Maurice creeps to the corner where the grandfather lies.

The grandfather is lying on his back, his hands folded across his chest like those of a dead man, his lips smiling.

And Maurice creeps back to his own corner and burrows under the ferns and heaps them over his head until not an inch of him can be seen.

DISSOLVE to

The room, in the light of morning, seen through cobwebs: through the cobwebbed window.

Padrig is rising, rumpling his hair and stretching. He goes across the room, through cobwebs, to the grandfather's corner, bends down and taps him on the shoulder.

Now we are inside the room.

PADRIG. The bright day is here.   Wake up, wake up, Grandfather
  O'Sullivan . . .

The old man is immediately awake.   He sits upright in bed.

THE GRANDFATHER. Good morning to ye, Padrig.

He puts out his hand for his pipe and matches on the floor near him.
Now Maurice is coming up slowly out of his refuge of ferns.
Padrig moves away.   We hear him whistling.
The grandfather looks across to where Maurice's head is visible
  among the ferns.

THE GRANDFATHER. And what were the delusions that came on
  you last night, Mirrisheen?
MAURICE (in wonder). You were asleep.   Can you hear what is
  said when you are sleeping?
THE GRANDFATHER. Never better.

Maurice scrambles out of the ferns, and stands brushing them off him
  in the middle of the room.
Still we hear Padrig's whistling.

MAURICE. Upon my word, they were no delusions at all, but I saw
  the long arm and the hand and I saw it take the rabbits off the
  nail. . . .
THE GRANDFATHER. Don't you know that no one dead would take
  the rabbits?

He is smoking happily now, a venerable old man sitting on the floor,
  up to his waist in ferns.

MAURICE. I don't know, but alive or dead he took them . . .
THE GRANDFATHER. And what is the living man on this island?

The whistling, off, stops.

PADRIG'S VOICE. Faith, Maurice, you were right.

Now, from the end of the room, we see Padrig standing at the open door, the bright morning and the wild fields behind him, holding a tin in his hand.

PADRIG. The rabbits are gone.   A sailor must have come ashore and taken them, and look, what did he do but slip a tin of tobacco under the door, as is the custom with them. . . .

MAURICE. Why didn't the dogs be barking outside?

THE GRANDFATHER. Dogs *like* sailors.

MAURICE. But what would a *living* sailor be doing on the Inish in the middle of the night?

THE GRANDFATHER (in the voice of a man ending an argument for once and for all). And what would a *dead* sailor be doing with tobacco. . . . We will set out now. . . .

And he jumps up out of the ferns, nimble as a young man. . . .

Now, in *LONG SHOT*, we see the grandfather, Maurice and Padrig walking through the thigh-deep grass of the Inish.

We hear the dogs barking.

We see the three figures bending every now and then and lifting up a rabbit and tying the rabbit on to the pole which Padrig carries across his back.   The pole is hung with rabbits like dark, furry washing on a line.

We see them on the edge of the cliff.

One by one, they go over the edge of the cliff.

Now there is nothing to be seen on Inish Vickallaun but the wild fern and grass blowing and the birds flying and crying over.

SYNOPSIS OF THE SECOND HALF OF
'TWENTY YEARS A-GROWING'

Here follows a sequence of a wake on the island. In this sequence we see, for the first time, the grown-up people of the island all
together drinking and story-telling. And we see the life of the
island for the last time through a child's eyes (for in the next sequence
Maurice has grown from childhood to adolescence). We see and
feel the fears of a child at the coming and the appearance of death.
His imagination is stirred by the stories of his grandfather at the wake:
stories of strange deaths and strange risings, stories as old as the island,
as old as Ireland, as old as peasants. And one of these stories we see
enacted: a short half-dream sequence to balance the first dream of the
butterfly and the skull.

After the drinking and the story-telling, the singing and the
keening, we *DISSOLVE* to the coffin being carried through the
island and down the windy paths to the sea. And as we see the
coffin descending, we hear the voice of Maurice O'Sullivan saying
that a part of him, too, died that night: a whole, deep part of his
life: his childhood.

Now we see a funeral procession of curraghs across the water as
we *FADE OUT*.

We *FADE INTO* a fine and sparkling morning on the island.
As the *CAMERA PANS* along the island we hear Maurice's voice
saying: 'Oh, it was a grand and lovely thing indeed, growing up by
that old loud sea, growing from a child into a youth. . . .' And
the *CAMERA* reaches Maurice as a youth. He is looking after
sheep on the cliffside, the sun yellowing in the west and a lark singing above. He sees lambs gambolling together.

And suddenly, over the brow of the cliff, appears a man. His coming-up is similar, in feeling and unexpectedness, to that of the King of the Island when Maurice first leaves Dingle and comes home. And just as the appearance of the King was the announcement to Maurice of a new and marvellous life, a life old as the hills and without any doubts at all, so the appearance of the man now announces the beginning of doubt, introduces into the idyllic timelessness of the island the first sound of the time-bound outer world and the first suggestion of adult responsibility.

The man is an Englishman. (In O'Sullivan's book he is George Thompson, the translator of *Twenty Years A-Growing.*)

The next sequence shows the growth of friendship between Maurice and the Englishman. Maurice is showing and explaining his own world; he is, in fact, putting forward the ageless argument for the dignity and beauty of life in the small peasant community. The Englishman is explaining *his* own world: paradise of money and the clock. (It should be mentioned here that the Englishman will *not* be made an unsympathetic character: he is not the serpent in the garden but the voice of the world beyond the Blasket horizon. He is the voice that is heard in all man's growing up. 'There is a world beyond your own,' that voice has always said.)

And now we see life on the island from Maurice's new viewpoint. We see him trying to adjust his new ideas to the peasant tradition. We see and hear the inevitable conflict: shall he remain on the island, knowing that the life of small peasant communities is noble and suffering, dignified and poor, beautiful and bitter, or shall he go into the wide, unknown world, forsaking his tradition?

And we build his relationship with Mauraid, now a child no longer but a young girl. And the conflict of ideas and the love of boy and girl rise together to a climax. Through all Maurice's adolescent life we are watching the departure of youth from the island, discontent and emigration. And the climax comes with Mauraid's decision to go to America along with the rest; and her going.

Now Maurice, of all the young people, of all those whom we saw in the happy early sequence, is alone on the island.

The Englishman appears again, to introduce the final argument. His is the voice of the outer world, the voice and the call, not necessarily of America but even of the outer world of Ireland itself. This voice and call are strengthened, in Maurice's mind, by his wish to join Mauraid. But against this is his own conviction of the rightness and the goodness of life on the island. And this conviction is expressed for him, finally, by the grandfather; by the enduring figure, the eternal peasant.

And Maurice remains upon the island. He faces poverty, privation, labour and loneliness; he faces a life without Mauraid and without help; but he is sure.

A DREAM OF WINTER...

This poem was written as a series of legends for eight winter pictures appearing in the magazine Lilliput X, No. 1 (*January, 1942*), pages *65–72. Each of the three-line stanzas appeared with the pertinent picture; in sequence these were: (1) trees, (2) frozen beach, (3) polar bear, (4) skiers, (5) statues, (6) city canal, (7) climbing glaciers, and (8) city snow scene.*

Very often on winter nights the halfshaped moonlight sees
Men through a window of leaves and lashes marking gliding
Into the grave an owl-tongued childhood of birds and cold trees,

Or drowned beyond water in the sleepers' fish-trodden churches
Watching the cry of the sea as snow flies sparkling, riding,
The ice lies down shining, the sandgrains skate on the beeches.

Often she watches through men's midnight windows, their winter
    eyes,
The conjured night of the North rain in a firework flood,
The Great Bear raising the snows of his voice to burn the skies.

And men may sleep a milkwhite path through the chill, struck still
    waves
Or walk on thunder and air in the frozen, birdless wood
On the eyelid of the North where only the silence moves,

Asleep may stalk among lightnings and hear the statues speak,
The hidden tongue in the melting garden sing like a thrush
And the soft snow drawing a bellnote from the marble cheek,

Drowned fast asleep beyond water and sound may mark the street
Ghost-deep in lakes where the rose-cheeked nightmare glides like a
    fish,
The Ark drifts on the cobbles, the darkness sails in a fleet,

Or, lying down still, may clamber the snow-exploded hill
Where the caverns hide the snowbull's ivory splinter,
Fossil spine of the sea-boned seal, iceprint of pterodactyl.

Oh birds, trees, fish and bears, singing statues, Arkfloods and seals
Steal from the sleeper awake as he waits in the winter
Morning, alone in his world, staring at the London wheels.

THE LONDON MODEL FOR
DYLAN THOMAS'S *UNDER MILK WOOD*

by Ralph Maud

The script by Dylan Thomas, 'The Londoner' written in 1946,[1] contributes a major item to the complicated history of *Under Milk Wood*. The biography of the town of Llaregyb takes us back beyond the Boat House days to pre-war Laugharne, when the Thomases lived successively at 'Eros' (on Gosport Street), at 'Sea View' and, temporarily, at Laugharne Castle owned by Richard Hughes. Hughes remembers a night in 1939 when he and Thomas took part in some amateur theatrical performance and decided afterwards that Laugharne itself, played by itself, would have made a much more entertaining evening.[2] Before Llaregyb there was 'Llareggub,' the name of the play as it was first printed,[3] a name which goes right back to Swansea 1934 and a story appropriately called 'Anagram' in manuscript, later to become 'The Orchards.'[4] After all, Dylan Thomas grew up among 'reverend madmen'[5] in a Welsh seaside town. More than Swansea, more even than Laugharne, the place which fits *Under Milk Wood* topographically is New Quay, Cardiganshire, where Thomas spent the period September 1944 to September 1945 and where he wrote 'Quite Early One Morning' for B.B.C. Wales (recorded 14 December 1944; broadcast 31 August 1945). The kernel of the idea as well as some of the characters and phraseology of Thomas's 'Play for Voices' were fashioned once and for all in New Quay. It is appropriate to add that the area around New Quay is the setting for Caradoc Evans's biting sketches of rural Welsh life; his play *Taffy*, scornful where *Under Milk Wood* is kind, is an analogue if not a model.[6] Perhaps the only real model for *Under Milk Wood* is the one Thomas himself constructed in the script for the B.B.C. General Overseas Service of 15 July 1946.

'The Londoner,' the thirteenth in a series 'This Is London' produced by R. D. Smith, is a model for *Under Milk Wood* in the basic sense that it works, dramatically, in a similar though more primitive manner. It presents a day in the life of a family and a neighborhood. The perspective of the outside world on the microcosm of Shepherds Bush[7] is provided by the Voice of Encyclopedia. These outsiders, prototypes of the Voice of a Guidebook in *Under Milk Wood*, are answered by the Voice of an Old Resident, an untraveled Captain Cat. As in *Under Milk Wood*, a Narrator presides over the day, which begins with dreams somewhat less Freudian than those of the repressed Welsh.

In the rather undistinguished scenes that follow the dream sequences, Thomas must have had his overseas audience in mind, one he judged more curious than critical. Only when we hear Lily alone in the kitchen after breakfast, after Ted has gone to work and the children to school, does the script approach something like the imaginative quality of *Under Milk Wood*—the rhyme helps, as does the name Lily, reminding us of Lily Smalls.

LILY. Empty the teapot—must have a new one—
      only this morning the kitchen was *so* neat—
      soak the frying pan—wish it wasn't fish—
      oh why do people have to eat—

      . . . .

      hope Ted's not tired of stews—
      got my basket and the doorkey?—
      and now I'm ready for the queues.

The script continues at a pedestrian speed through shopping scene, cafe scene, pub scene, children in bed scene, until the Narrator can complete the circle with: 'It is a summer night now in Montrose Street. And the street is sleeping. In number 49, all is quiet. The Jacksons are dreaming.' Thus, this radio play parallels, with less interesting suburban events, the dramatic movement from dawn to dusk in *Under Milk Wood.*

The apparent ease with which this script fell into the mold makes clear that the full day as a basic dramatic unit of time was congenial to Thomas, though he had occasional pangs at being so plotless. Daniel Jones' Preface to *Under Milk Wood* tells of Thomas's desire for a more ambitious plot for the play: his town was to be literally on trial, with Captain Cat as Counsel for the Defence. The Prosecution's final speech was to have given a minute description of a sane town, upon which the people of Llaregub would immediately withdraw their defence and beg to be cordoned off from such a world.[8] Ingenious enough; but one has no regrets that Thomas was unable to fit his materials into this plot. If he was, in John Davenport's words, 'incapable of dramatic structure'[9] at least he had found a minimum of structure that would be satisfying to himself and to his audiences. The single day is the ordinary unit of ordinary existence; any additional plotting would be bound to introduce an extra-ordinary story. This simplest of structuring, already implicit in the dawn scene of 'Quite Early One Morning,' was required in order to make a unified play from its tableaux in verse.[10] In the radio script of 1946 we can see Thomas trying out the effectiveness of the normal day as a dramatic unit, practising on Londoners before applying the idea, with all the added assurance and skill, to his beloved Welsh.

Simon Fraser University, Burnaby, British Columbia.

NOTES

[1] I am indebted to the British Broadcasting Corporation and the Trustees of the Dylan Thomas Estate for permission to quote passages from this script.

[2] Richard Hughes in a letter to T. H. Jones in T. H. Jones, *Dylan Thomas* (Edinburgh and London, 1963), pp. 89–92. *Under Milk Wood* was first performed in Laugharne, with an amateur cast, in August 1958.

[3] 'Llareggub (A piece for Radio Perhaps),' *Botteghe Oscure*, IX (1952).

[4] 'Anagram' (or 'Mr. Tritas On The Roofs') is dated October 1934 in a MS Notebook at the Lockwood Library of the State University of New York at Buffalo. 'The Orchards' was published in *Criterion* (July 1936) and subsequently in Dylan Thomas, *A Prospect of the Sea* (London, 1955), where 'Llareggub' is found on p. 82.

[5] Ibid. 'The Town that was Mad,' a working title for *Under Milk Wood*, was used as late as 5 September 1952 in a letter to Mr. Layton of the B.B.C.

[6] Thomas's two visits to Caradoc Evans are recorded in Oliver Sandys, *The Miracle Stone of Wales* (London, 1957), p. 14, and Glyn Jones, 'Dylan Thomas—The Other Man,' *Western Mail* (23 April 1958), p. 6. On first going up to London, Thomas regaled new acquaintances with 'uninterrupted praise' of Caradoc Evans's books (recounted in a letter to A. E. Trick, about December 1934). While acknowledging the poet's affection for the older Anglo-Welsh writer, one may dispute that any particular character is 'derived' from Caradoc Evans (see T. H. Jones, p. 93).

[7] From time to time in his bachelor days Thomas stayed at Norman Cameron's flat in Hammersmith, the London suburb adjacent to Shepherds Bush.

[8] Preface to Dylan Thomas, *Under Milk Wood* (London, 1954), p. vii.

[9] In *Dylan Thomas: The Legend and the Poet*, ed. E. W. Tedlock (London, 1960), p. 80.

[10] One is reminded of similar tableaux in Edgar Lee Masters' *Spoon River Anthology*, another literary analogue. Thomas's pragmatic interest in *Spoon River Anthology* dates from before January 1951; his B.B.C. talk on Masters appears in *Harper's Bazaar* (June 1963).

"THE LONDONER"

ANNOUNCER. "When a man is tired of London," said Dr. Johnson, "he is tired of life, for there is in London all that life can afford." We present the last in our series, "This is London". "The Londoner", written and narrated by Dylan Thomas and produced by R. D. Smith.

Bow Bells.

NARRATOR. A day in the life of Mr. and Mrs. Jackson, Ted and Lily, of number forty nine Montrose Street, Shepherds Bush, London, West 12.

QUESTIONER. Where is Shepherds Bush?

NARRATOR. It is a busy inner-suburban centre, on one of the main west roads out of London. It is part of the borough of Hammersmith. It is a difficult district to describe, because it is neither a part of the mass of central London nor is it an outer suburb with its own separate identity, it is, rather, a . . .

QUESTIONER. And what is Montrose Street? What does it look like?

VOICE OF AN EXPERT. It is a grey-bricked street of one hundred houses. Built in 1890. Two bedrooms, a front room and a kitchen. Bathrooms were built into less than half of the houses in 1912. A scullery and a backyard. Rent 28 shillings. Too cold in the winter, too hot in the summer. Ugly, inconvenient, and infinitely depressing.

VOICE OF AN OLD RESIDENT. No, no. You got it all wrong. It's a nice, lively street. There's all the shops you want at one end, and there's pubs at both ends. Mightn't be much to look at, but there's always things going on, there's always something to see, buses and trams and lorries and prams and kids and dogs and dogfights sometimes and . . .

QUESTIONER. And who are Mr. and Mrs. Jackson, Ted and Lily? How old are they? What do they look like?

ALFRED. Ted works for a builder's firm, Sedgman and Parker. Him and me—I'm his mate, Alfred—we're demolishing air-raid shelters. He's about thirty five. He looks like . . . well, he's about average height, he's got kind of darkish brown hair, it's not *really* dark though, and kind of ordinary brownish eyes as far as I can remember, he looks like . . . well, he looks like Ted Jackson.

MRS. COOLEY. Lily's what's known as a housewife. That's what you put on all the forms you got to sign before you can call your name your own and then you can't. Housewife! Slaving morn noon and night and never a word of gratitude. And all for *men*! She's about thirty two. She's fair. I suppose some men'd call her pretty but then of course I'm a woman and I live next door. Oh, she'd pass in a crowd . . . she's very sweet, I will say that for her . . .

QUESTIONER. Are there any children?

SCHOOLTEACHER. Two. They both attend the school of which I am head-teacher. Carole, aged 12. Len, aged 10.

Disc.

NARRATOR. It's nearly half past six on a summer morning. Montrose Street is awake.

Noise of Cars and Lorries.

NARRATOR. But most of the houses are still sleeping. In number 49, all is quiet. Lily Jackson is dreaming.

Music.

LILY. Ooh, what a beautiful dress . . . like the one Ingrid Bergman was wearing in what-was-the-name . . . And the music! Lovelier than oh-I-can't-remember, the one with the violin and the big sad eyes. Look, they're walking down the aisle, white as Christmas. There's lights all over the place like victory night. Oh, it's all changing. They're dancing in a kind of palace now . . .

214

Look, there's Mrs. Cooley next door with a dustcap on . . .
They're singing . . . I'm there too . . . I'm dancing on the falling
snow . . . Where's Ted . . . where's Ted?

Music.

NARRATOR. Ted Jackson is dreaming.

TED. "All right then, come outside". . . "Don't you go outside with
Ted Jackson he's champion of the world". . . right left right left
short-arm jab . . . why am I lying here in the rain behind the
barbed wire . . . there's a single drop of blood on Lily's photo . . .
Right left right left right uppercut . . . Mr. Jackson, may I present
you with this road-drill made out of pure gold in honour of . . .
There goes the bell for the millionth round . . .

Alarm Clock Rings.

NARRATOR. Number forty nine Montrose Street is awake. Lily
Jackson is in the kitchen.

Kitchen Noises: Noise of Frying.

LILY. . . . ever such a funny dream, Ted . . . oh dear, where's the
teacaddy gone, I know I put it down . . . here it is . . . I was in a
kind of church and then, you know what it's like when you're
dreaming, it wasn't a church it was a kind of palace and Mrs.
Cooley next door was there in a dustcap and a bathing-
costume . . .

TED. That old barrage balloon . . .

LILY. Go on, you know you'd like to have seen her . . .

TED. I'd like to see Mrs. Cooley floating in with a couple of real
eggs and some fried liver and . . .

LILY. Here's your tea . . .

TED. . . . and sausages that aren't made out of old newspaper and
minced shaving brushes . . . Pictures tonight?

LILY. If I can get Mrs. Cooley to keep an eye on the house . . .

TED. Mrs. Cooley'll be living here soon . . . Keep her moored in
the backyard . . .

215

LILY. . . . and then I was dancing in the palace, in my dream I mean, and I said to Mrs. Cooley "Where's Ted?" and then before I knew where I was we were all in somewhere like Kew Gardens only I saw the 11 bus too . . . Oh, I'm losing everything this morning. Wish we had a nice modern kitchen you could put your hand on anything . . .

Scraping of Chair.

LILY. Don't forget your sandwiches. 'Bye, darling . . .
TED. (*at door*) Hope *my* bus don't go through Kew Gardens . . .
NARRATOR. And he catches the workman's bus . . . Who's the conductor this morning? Tom Fletcher? Charlie Preston?

Door Slamming.

Traffic.

Bus Drawing Up.

TED. Morning, Charlie . . .
CONDUCTOR. Morning, Ted . . .

Bus Moving Off.

Bus Noise Background.

Men's Voices in Bus.

WORKMAN. Black Boy closed again last night.
ALFRED. . . . Get their supplies Wednesday . . . Open seven to nine every night except Monday and Tuesday.
TED. You should open an information bureau, Alfred, shouldn't he.
WORKMAN. I walked a mile and a half for a shandy . . . and no fags either . . .
ALFRED. Always get fags in the Carpenters' Arms . . .
TED. Information supplied free about every pub from here to Barnes.
ALFRED. Well you got to look after yourself haven't you?
WORKMAN. And only *half* a shandy too . . .
NARRATOR. There are different kinds of worries in Lily's kitchen.

Kitchen Noises.

216

LILY. (*at door*) Come on, Len. Come on, Carole. Breakfast's ready.

CAROLE. (*from upstairs*) Mummy, Len's floating ships in the basin . . .

LILY. Come on both of you or it'll get cold . . .

CAROLE. (*from upstairs*) Mummy, Len's throwing water at me . . .

LILY. Stop it at once, Len . . . Oh, dear.

Noise Children Running Downstairs.

CAROLE. And he said a rude word and he said . . .

LILY. Sit down at once, both of you, I don't want to hear what Len said and I don't want to hear anybody telling tales either . . . You're one as bad as the other . . .

LEN. Tell tale, tell tale . . .

LILY. Eat up now, you're late . . .

CAROLE. Mummy, why can't I wear my hair long and straight and half of it right across my face so that I look out mysterious . . .

LILY. You've got nice curly hair, you don't want to make it straight and you don't want to look mysterious either . . .

LEN. If Carole's going to have her hair all silly like that, can I go bald then . . .

LILY. Eat your breakfast and don't talk so daft.

LEN. Bald like Uncle Vernon . . .

LILY. If Uncle Vernon heard you talk like that . . . and eat properly, Carole, don't put your finger in your porridge, what d'you think spoons are for?

LEN. Eating jelly.

LEN. (*at door*) Goodbye, mummy.

CAROLE. 'Bye, mummy.

LILY. Goodbye, darlings . . . Don't run across the road.

Door Slamming.

LILY. Oh dear, sometimes I think they'll be the death of me if they didn't look so pretty when they were being naughty. Not that they're really very pretty I suppose, to anyone else except Ted and me: of course, Carole's got very good colouring and *lovely* hair,

217

and she's got quite the sweetest eyes I ever saw, and good features, too: and of course boys are different, I mean they don't *have* to be goodlooking, but there isn't any boy in the street that's half as intelligent and he's got such a *wicked* smile . . . Oh dear, I suppose there never *were* such children . . . all mothers are the same. Len looks like Ted must have looked when he was a little boy. Just like in that photograph his mother showed me, the one she wouldn't part with for anything, in a sailor's suit with a funny hat and smiling just like he does now when he's trying to get his own way . . .

MRS. COOLEY. (*off*)   Are you in, dear?

LILY. Oh come in, Mrs. Cooley, I was standing here all by myself day-dreaming and all the washing-up to be done and housework and shopping and everything . . .

MRS. COOLEY. The back was open so I just dropped in for a moment.   Mrs. Mackenzie twenty three's gone to hospital, I saw the ambulance.

LILY. Poor Mrs. Mackenzie . . .

MRS. COOLEY. Well, my dear, we all knew it wasn't long before she'd got to, and I was saying to Mrs. Mizler, if there's one thing you can't afford to play with, that's your health, and the way Mrs. Mackenzie was going on everyone knew it was only a matter of months . . . I told her at the beginning of the summer . . . I said, pains like you're suffering, Mrs. Mackenzie, aren't natural . . . but there, the very next day she was going to the West End for a little jaunt with three children under seven and Mrs. Walker from King Street who should know better . . .

LILY. Poor Mrs. Mackenzie.   Is anyone looking after the children now she's in hospital?

MRS. COOLEY. That's just what I'm going over to see myself . . . but I thought I'd drop in for a moment and tell you the news and ask you if you could spare some salt until tomorrow, there's not a pinch in the house and really I can't go up to the shops now with having to look at poor Mrs. Mackenzie's children and everything and as I thought you wouldn't mind . . .

NARRATOR. Of course they don't mind in the kitchens of Montrose street . . . sharing and sharing alike with bits of things . . . with keeping an eye on the children . . . with trying to keep life friendly and straight. They're women working together . . . just as Ted is working now, with Alfred and Stanley and the rest of them . . . working on demolition.

Noise of Drills and Demolition. Fade Noise into background.

ALFRED. Gives you a funny feeling, knocking down air-raid shelters. I helped to build this one.

WORKMAN. Looks a bit ricketty, too . . .

TED. I used to make wireless sets and as soon as I'd finished 'em I'd pull 'em to bits. Always. Must have made scores of sets and never listened in more than a couple of minutes.

ALFRED. That's different.

TED. 'Course it's different. I used to try to get Moscow and South America on sets I made. Only got Germany on air-raid shelters. But I learned something new all the time I was fiddling about with coils and condensers and things. There was some point pull-ing them to bits and starting again . . .

A Crash.

ALFRED. One for old Hitler . . .

Another Crash.

WORKMAN. One for old Franco . . .

TED. . . . Hope we all learned something new now. Knock all the shelters and pillboxes to bits, and start all over again. But not to build new shelters. We've had enough of that.

ALFRED. Don't no need no shelters for atom-bombs. Give me a nice old fashioned 200 pounder.

TED. If a bomb had your name on it, you had it coming and that's all. Atom-bombs got everyruddybody's name on 'em, that's the difference. But there aren't going to be any atom bombs. There can't be. It doesn't make sense. We're not children.

ALFRED. I feel young enough sometimes, on a Saturday night.

TED. No, I mean, *we*'re the Government, aren't we. It's we who got to say, "No, there's not going to be any funny business any more." And just *see* that there isn't either. If people all over the world say, "We don't want atom bombs, we want all the things that atomic energy can make not what it can bust up," then that's how it's going to be.

ALFRED. You shouldn't talk politics when you're working . . .

TED. If a man can't talk politics when he's got a pneumatic drill in his hand, when can he then . . .

Up Noise of Drills etc.: Music While You Work.

NARRATOR. Mrs. Lily Jackson is working too.

LILY. Empty the teapot—must have a new one—
only this morning the kitchen was *so* neat—
soak the frying-pan—wish it wasn't fish—
oh *why* do people have to eat—
Why do men put fag ends in their saucers—
knives and forks and plates and cups—
think of all the breakfasts in Montrose Street—
and think of all the washing-ups—
I won't scrub the floor this morning—
I wish the plumber'd come about the sink—
I'll just sweep the breadcrumbs up and then—
another cup of tea I think . . .
Woman shouldn't grumble, only to themselves,
Mother always used to say—
now it's make the beds and tidy up the bedrooms—
oh, the same thing every day—
clear up after the children—
they fling their clothes *any*where—
and the *mess* they make in the bathroom—
I think there's time to do my hair—
Wish I had a proper hair-do—
found a grey hair yesterday—
troubles and grey hairs never come singly

mother always used to say—
And now it's nearly time for shopping—
Let's see, is my hat all right?—
and the new points begin *next* Monday—
have a look in my purse—bit tight
but I *think* I'll manage if I'm careful—
hope Ted's not tired of stews—
got my basket and the doorkey?—
and now I'm all ready for the queues.

Noise of Traffic.

Women's Voices Background: Chatter.

1ST SHOPPER. Last week there was bananas in Humphries . . . saw them with my own eyes . . .

2ND SHOPPER. Keeps 'em for his regular customers, so he says . . .

1ST SHOPPER. All gone when I got there, of course . . .

2ND SHOPPER. If I'm not a regular customer, Mr. Humphries, I said, who is then? Mrs. Miniver?

1ST SHOPPER. That's right, dear . . .

3RD SHOPPER. Pity the men can't queue a bit . . .

1ST SHOPPER. How long you been queuing, dear?

3RD SHOPPER. I've been here half an hour.

2ND SHOPPER. I been queuing for six and a half years.

4TH SHOPPER. You're right there, too, why shouldn't the men do their bit of queuing? They eat most don't they?

LILY. Oh, men have got to line up too, give them their dues . . . buses, and tobacco, and . . .

2ND SHOPPER. It's all right for you to be so considerate, you're two in front of me . . .

1ST SHOPPER. Still, mustn't grumble . . .

2ND SHOPPER. Ho! Mustn't grumble, hear that, Mrs. Armstrong! Who's grumbling? Everything's *lovely*. Mind your cabbage, Flo . . .

Up Noise of Woman Grumbling.

NARRATOR. But you must be polite in the grocer's . . .

LILY. How much does all that come to, Mr. Brookes?

MR. BROOKES. Let's see now—that'll be

LILY. I don't suppose it's worth my asking if you've got such a thing as a jelly, Mr. Brookes? You know what children are in this hot weather and . . .

MR. BROOKES. Show me a jelly, Mrs. Jackson, anywhere in the shop, you can have it, you can have it free, I'd be *pleased* to see a jelly, I'd be *delighted* . . . do you know, Mrs. Jackson, I'm not telling you a word of a lie when I tell you my wife's *mad* for a jelly but . . .

NARRATOR. And so on, and so on . . . and—on to the butcher's.

BUTCHER. Offal, Mrs. Jackson? Now you're asking. As far as *I* can see, animals don't possess no insides these days, worth mentioning . . .

Noise of Road-Drills etc. Fade.

NARRATOR. Ted Jackson's gang has broken off for lunch. They are sitting in Joe's Eating House: the Komfy. It is one long, narrow room, opening on the street, with cubicles on each side, and in each cubicle is a wooden bench and a plain wooden table. On the walls, pre-war notices which nobody has bothered to take down, announce unobtainable food. The men are drinking large cups of dark brown tea, their parcels and tin boxes open beside them.

ALFRED. My daughter says, what'll happen when there's television in every house? Won't there be any more cinemas then? My daughter says, when her young man asks her to go to the pictures, all they'll do is go and sit in the parlour with his old man and the missus. How can they hold hands then?

TED. You tell your daughter—who's her young man now? young Arthur?—there'll always be communal places, there'll always be . . .

ALFRED. My daughter don't want communal places, Ted, she wants to go to the pictures. No, young Arthur's finished. It's young Herbie Phillips now, the chap who was a prisoner of war.

You know, the chap who used to be errand boy for Wilson's and then the next we heard of him he was a commando. Funny, isn't it.

WORKMAN. Wonder if they let him keep his tricycle . . .

TED. There was a chap who was a prisoner with me—used to be a shopwalker in one of these big stores I've forgotten which. You know, "this way to the underwear, Madam" . . . and there he was with a damned great bayonet scar half across his face . . . wonder what he's doing now . . . what's a chap like that do, scar or no scar, when *he* comes back? No shops for him again: he was one of the toughest fellows I ever saw . . . he used to sit there half the day, just staring, and moving his great torn fingers just like *this* . . . as though he were trying to strangle something . . .

WORKMAN. How long was you a prisoner?

TED. Three years. One year on my back, flat out, and two years thinking . . .

ALFRED. Funny when it's so hard to get soap that that's what old Joe puts in the tea, isn't it. That's what it tastes like . . .

TED. I used to think about things I didn't *know* I knew . . . things used to come into my head that I knew I wasn't clever enough to think . . . but they came all right. I'm in the building trade, I used to say to myself, I'm married, I live in Shepherds Bush, I got two kids, I'm not a philosopher, I used to say . . . I'm a Londoner, I am . . .

NARRATOR. Lily Jackson is having *her* lunch alone in the tidy kitchen. The kids are having their lunch at school—Lily's made a cup of tea for herself and a sandwich. She's looking through the window at the grey small square of garden where the clothes are blowing on the line. Beyond them are the roofs of the world.

LILY. Three years were an awful long time. Oh, every time I thought how long they were for me, I knew, I knew they were longer for Ted. Before they said on the wireless he was a prisoner of war, oh long before, I knew he wasn't dead. I never had to tell lies to myself, like poor Sally Peters up the street. I knew he was thinking of me. I used to hear his voice in the silly old dance tunes they played on the wireless, but the words weren't silly any more. "I love you, darling mine," was always him saying it to me. "In the silence of my lonely room I think of you, night and day," he used to say. Oh I knew he wasn't alone, all right, there were thousands and thousands. But they were all alone too. Walking down Montrose Street with Carole and Len, he was walking with me. I remembered everything he ever said to me from the day we met in the dance hall down Hammersmith till the day he asked me to marry him and I couldn't say yes or any-thing because people were looking at us in the park and then an old man sat down next to us on the bench and said it was very cold for August, and he couldn't understand why we both burst out laughing and went on laughing and laughing till we nearly cried, and then Ted kissed me, kissed me with the old man staring, and then the old man said, "and what's more it's going to rain . . ."

Knock on Door.

Gwen. (*at door*) Anyone at home?
Lily. Come in, Gwen love. Take your things off.
Gwen. Don't be silly. I've only got a summer frock on.
Lily. Well come and sit down in the front room, the kitchen's like an oven . . .
Gwen. Just for a minute then . . .
Lily. I haven't seen you for weeks, Gwen . . . Willy okay?
Gwen. Same as usual. Trying to get some back pay from the Army. I just wondered if you're not too busy you'd like to come down the Broadway. I got two coupons left and I want to buy a pair of black gloves . . .
Lily. Gwen, whatever for?
Gwen. Willy's Auntie Beryl's died—you know, the one who gave us the dinner-set—and the funeral's tomorrow. I haven't got any-thing black at all only that grey dress I had last winter.
Lily. No I can't come really. I've got such a lot of mending and they'll be out of a school in an hour and there's ironing too . . .
Gwen. Oh come on, I'll stand you an ice . . .

224

LILY. I'll have to spend the whole evening mending if I do . . . oh, all right then . . . perhaps I'll catch a glimpse of Ted . . . he *hates* me watching him working . . .

GWEN. Well, you know where he is, anyway . . . Once Willy's gone off in the lorry, heaven only knows . . .

Noise of Traffic.

LILY. You do look funny wearing black gloves with that cotton dress . . . put them in your bag, Gwen . . .

GWEN. Go on with you, I'm making a new fashion . . . Not bad for four and eleven three is it? Where shall we have our ice?

LILY. Let's buy one off that chap over there . . . look, there's choc ices . . .

GWEN. What, me with a choc ice and my black gloves on? Think of my colour scheme! Okay. Two please.

LILY. Makes me feel like a kid walking along the street with a wafer in my hand . . .

GWEN. Go on, you don't look so old anyway . . . not a day over sixty . . .

LILY. Oh, look, look! There's Ted.

GWEN. Where?

LILY. On top of that old shelter there . . .

GWEN. Well if it isn't! Making a nice little ruin isn't he?

Noise of Drills.

ALFRED. Don't look now, Ted, but there's a young woman waving at you . . . Blimey, there's *two* young women waving now . . .

Up Noise of Drills: Noise of Traffic Background.

GWEN. Here we are then. Forty nine. Nice of you to have come with me, Lil.

LILY. Thanks for the ice.

GWEN. Give my love to brother Ted. I'll come along and see you next week.

LILY. Bye-bye then.

GWEN. Abyssinyia . . .

LILY. And don't throw your books everywhere, Len. Put them in the cupboard.

LEN. Can I go out on my bike now, ma?

LILY. Yes, and don't call me ma.

CAROLE. Why don't you like being called ma, mummy?

LILY. Because it's common. Now if you've finished your tea you can help me take the clothes off the line . . .

CAROLE. Yes, ma.

Noise of Whistles and Sirens.

NARRATOR. Now, for Ted Jackson, the working day is over; dusty and tired, he waits for his bus, in a queue. Newspaper placards announce a shocking murder: The Cabinet meets again: a film-star has 'flu: a West End play has been running for fifteen years: "Bishop says shame to mixed bathing in the Sea": the weather is forecasted, firmly, as dry, or wet: nobody scored at Lords. And a workman wants his tea.

Kitchen Noises.

TED. I can do with it, too . . . old Alfred nearly fell off the wall when he saw you waving.

LILY. More stew?

TED. Yes please. It isn't a stew, it's a kind of a pie. Shepherds Bush pie, that what it is? And waving ice-cream too and Alfred and me like a couple of pieces of hot-buttered toast.

CAROLE. How could you look like toast?

TED. Don't be so literal. How's Gwen?

LILY. She's burying Willy's Auntie Beryl tomorrow.

TED. Dead, I hope?

CAROLE. I'm not so literal, I was only asking.

LILY. Oh, dear, I do like your jokes, Ted. Here's a fresh cup. Both of them.

TED. Len out on his bike? He better be careful. Saw him a couple of evenings ago racing that young Larkin's boy down by old Hawk Road. Asking for it. Pictures night tonight?

LILY. I got all that mending to do, *and* the ironing, I told Gwen if I went out with her I'd have to stay in and do it. You better go and see if there's any beer in the Black Boy.

TED. There's many a husband never heard his wife say that to him since the day they were married. Or before. Better tell Len. I'll fix that pump of his when I get back.

CAROLE. I wish there was a Black Boy for girls.

LILY. Oh Carole!

NARRATOR. And for Carole and Len the day is over. Now they must go to bed. But in the Black Boy, that favourite public house, the evening is just beginning.

BARMAID. Evening, Mr. Dollery. No bitter. Only mild and bitter. Evening, Mr. Jackson.

MR. DOLLERY. Be mean with the mild then . . .

TED. Evening, Dora. Pint of what you got. Evening, Mr. Dollery.

MR. DOLLERY. 'Lo, Ted. Makes a chap think, doesn't it . . .

CUSTOMER. Old Stanley's gone to bed till there's Burton.

MR. DOLLERY. Seen they got a new dartboard, Ted? I been measuring. The double nineteen's eighth of an inch too narrow.

TED. Too low for me. Give me the twenties. Funny thing, when we made a dartboard once in the camp none of us could remember which way the numbers went . . .

CUSTOMER. Burton's proper beer, Stanley says. Bitter's drinking . . .

MR. DOLLERY. Eighth of a inch too narrow!

TED. . . . You know, so long since we played. We made a shove-halfpenny board too. You had to hit the halfpennies with a hammer and then they'd go up and down like a Giant Racer.

MR. DOLLERY. You only got to breathe on the board I had once . . .

TED. Same again?

MR. DOLLERY. Ta. You only got to *breathe* on the board and there they were: all five halfpennies in Annie's bed. Cheerioh.

TED. Cheerioh.

CUSTOMER. You can't job old Stanley off with mild and bitter.

TED. Closing at nine?

MR. DOLLERY. Or before. Depends on the dart team. If they don't come in there'll be beer enough. But if they do come in they'll finish the beer and then they won't be able to finish their game. So they don't know what to do, if you see what I mean.

Up Men's Voices.

CUSTOMER. (*with morose satisfaction*) They're having an argey-bargey . . .

TED. What's the fuss, Dora?

BARMAID. Oh, one of 'em's saying you can't be a boxer if you drink and the other one's saying you ought to train on quarts and . . .

NEW CUSTOMER. (*pugnaciously*) Look at me. I been drinking beer heavy every day of my life, year in, year out . . .

TED. Yes, but does it help your boxing?

NEW CUSTOMER. Boxing? Never boxed in my life. I'm an invalid.

Up Pub Noises.

NARRATOR. Carole and Len are in bed. In the kitchen, in the last light of the day, Lily and Ted are sitting quietly, together and alone. Lily is sewing.

TED. This was one of the things I used to remember. The kids are upstairs asleep; Carole's got a doll on her pillow, it's only got one arm and the sawdust runs out of its head; at the bottom of Len's bed there's soldiers and a bear and a kind of duck that makes the wrong noise when you press it: miaow, like a cat. I remembered that all right. And you and me were sitting downstairs, just like we are now. You could *hear* the chaps all round you, thinking, as they lay down with their eyes wide open. Some with their mouths wide open too, snorting like Spitfires. Dreaming away.

LILY. (*softly*) You're half asleep now . . .

TED. All of us thinking about home. Sentimental. Nobody called nobody sentimental then . . .

LILY. You're half asleep . . .

TED. (*as if dreaming*) Things used to come into my head I didn't know I could think—but they came all right. I'm not a philosopher, I used to say, I'm in the building trade. Ted Jackson, thirty-five, 49 Montrose Street, Shepherds Bush, married, two children, wife's name Lily . . . Lily . . .

LILY. Let's go to bed.

Music.

NARRATOR. It is a summer night now in Montrose Street. And the street is sleeping. In number forty nine, all is quiet. The Jacksons are dreaming.